Praise for *The Northbound Train*

"Karl has outlined a compelling description of how to develop and deliver customer value. A 'must-read' for anyone who wants to stay in business."

—Anders Franson
Manager Commercial Development
Volvo Cars of North America

"Karl Albrecht's comprehensive book explores future trends in the business world and what successful companies will need to concentrate on to survive and prosper. It will encourage many executives to think and rethink their company's future direction."

—Ken Blanchard, Ph.D.
co-author of *The One-Minute Manager*

"With today's trend in both the private and public sectors toward a fundamental refocusing on customers, this book provides a thoroughly helpful approach to the reengineering of what business we do and how we can best do it."

—Noel Tanzer
Secretary/CEO
Commonwealth Dept. of the Arts, Australia

"Outstanding. Practical, eye-opening observations. I want to go back and read it again. Albrecht's work continues to excel."

—Carole Presley
Sr. VP Marketing, Federal Express

"Albrecht manages to cleanly connect the sometimes elusive notion of 'vision' to the most fundamental of business issues— creating value for customers."

—John Guaspari, VP, Rath & Strong

"Leadership takes an inspiring vision that can be shared, understood, and discussed by the organization. In this new book, Karl Albrecht develops in depth the need for a vision and a charter for setting out an organization's destiny."

—Goran Carstedt, CEO, IKEA North America

"I love the way Albrecht puts 'customer value' right at the heart of the successful business vision, because that's exactly what business should always be about—delivering customer value."

"Wonderful! Albrecht's ideas represent the very best in state-of-the-art management thinking for the next century. Every executive and manager should read *The Northbound Train*. I intend to buy the first 500 copies for my top management staff."

"CEOs and managers must make *The Northbound Train* compulsory reading. . . . They will be 'without a ticket' unless they can successfully provide customer-focused leadership and develop committed, service-oriented teams. And how can they achieve all of that? It's in the book!"

The Northbound Train

Finding the Purpose
Setting the Direction
Shaping the Destiny of
Your Organization

Karl Albrecht

American Management Association

New York • Atlanta • Boston • Chicago • Kansas City • San Francisco • Washington, D.C.
Brussels • Mexico City • Tokyo • Toronto

Library of Congress Cataloging-in-Publication Data

Albrecht, Karl.
    The Northbound train : finding the purpose, setting the direction,
shaping the destiny of your organization / Karl Albrecht.
        p. cm.
    Includes bibliographical references and index.
    ISBN 0-8144-0233- X
    1. Organizational effectiveness.   2. Strategic planning.
3. Customer service.   I. Title.
HD58.9.A447   1994
658.4'012—dc20   93-49388
                                                              CIP

Printing number

10 9 8 7 6 5 4 3 2 1

Contents

Preface

No company is safely and permanently successful in today's business environment. For many organizations, perhaps most, doing business now has become a new game with new rules. For some, it has even become a struggle for survival.

The list of successful firms that have hit the skids in recent years reads like the proverbial who's who of international business. Even legendary giants like IBM, General Motors, Sears, Kodak, and Digital Equipment Corporation have astounded onlookers who thought they were the invincible stalwarts of commerce. The experience of recent years has wrecked some of the most basic assumptions about business success. If it can happen to them, it can happen to any company.

The rate of change in economies, markets, and industries is now outrunning the ability of the conventional corporate structure to keep up. *Shock waves* like the worldwide collapse of communism, the digital-electronic revolution, the Japanese "quality miracle," and the so-called age wave are powerful enough to change the very structure and the rules for doing business in some industries. "Let's get back to basics!" is a futile battle cry. The old basics no longer exist. We have to discover the new basics.

Every economic recession in recent years has generated a new wave of change, distorting and restructuring markets, industries, and even national economies. In many cases, the loss of tens of thousands of jobs is only partly due to sagging demand and more commonly due to the structural changes themselves. Many of those jobs will never return because the need for them has disappeared. But many others will come into being as a result of new opportunities and new ventures.

Business leaders are faced now more than at any time in the past with the need to define clearly—or increasingly to *re*define—their enterprises. The rising clamor about "vision," "mission," and "direction" signals a widening *crisis of meaning* among companies of all kinds, large and small. A remarkable number of firms seem to have only the vaguest sense of their own identity and uniqueness. Many don't really know who they are. Indeed, in industrialized countries like the United States, the crisis of meaning for organizations seems to mirror a corresponding crisis of meaning at the national level and even at the personal level.

The old success premise of "Get a good product, produce it at low cost, and sell it hard" is just too simplistic now. You have to know who you are, what you're really good at, what your basic business logic is, and what value-creation premise will win the business of your customers. In short, you must have a vision for your success and a direction for getting there. You have to know what train you're going to ride.

This book uses that metaphor of riding a train—the *Northbound Train*—as a focusing concept for creating the vision and meaning that can energize an organization and propel it toward its success. It is the leader who must choose the train, as a matter of careful thinking and strategy formulation. The leader must help people in the organization understand and commit to the vision. And the leader must help them learn to do what it takes to make the vision a reality.

All of this seems rather self-evident, but there is a huge gap between the concept and the reality. There is much more to defining an organizational vision and direction than simply sitting down and writing a few flowery phrases. In twenty years of working with organizations of almost every imaginable type, I've seen relatively few really powerful and meaningful corporate statements of vision, mission, or philosophy. Most are either vague, puffy, and meaningless, or dull, prosaic, and uninspiring. A very few actually have the power to move people.

Most executive teams have trouble articulating the driving

success premise of their enterprises, not because they can't compose flowery phrases, but because they don't *have* a driving premise. They haven't discerned the real meaning in what they do. With no compelling message to communicate, they're stuck with platitudes, homilies, and meaningless one-liners.

The existence (or lack) of a clear focus for success—the northbound train—sets the context for just about everything else that happens in and to the organization. Without it, leadership becomes a day-by-day struggle against seemingly isolated issues. People in such organizations merely work for a living, not for a higher purpose. Customer value becomes the hit-or-miss outcome of routine work activities, not a source of pride, creativity, and personal commitment.

A mind-set of control, caution, and scarcity leads to cost-obsessed management and consequently an impoverished customer value package that says figuratively, "We're nothing special." The vicious cycle of price competition conditions both customers and competitors to abandon all focus on total value and settle for price as the lowest common denominator of trade. Market differentiation goes out the window and the "product" or "service" becomes a commodity.

Contrast this with those few outstandingly successful firms that have made customer value their defining premise—their northbound train. They have evolved a compelling definition of who they are, what they do, and where they intend to go. They have turned the vicious cycle into a virtuous cycle: customer value leads to customer preference, which leads to customer retention, which enables them to continually build higher value, which leads to greater customer preference, and on it goes.

By concentrating their attention and resources on a single compelling business idea, they break the death grip of price-only warfare and even define the new rules of the game for their competitors.

Knowing the new rules of the game, these firms are moving beyond the boundaries and restrictions of the standard self-contained corporation as the traditional model for deploying resources. Understanding as they do that success in business is increasingly all about deploying knowledge and technology, they realize that partnering, networking, and leverage are becoming the keys to success. In a fast-changing business environment, fixed capital is becoming less of an asset and more of an encumbrance. By using knowledge and technology to leverage the capital and energies of others, they are moving toward the *value-creating enterprise* as the post-capitalist model for strategic success.

This book deals with the challenge and the enormous potential payoff involved in creating and implementing the northbound train concept for your enterprise. It's about vision, meaning, and strategy, as well as the leadership that's essential in building a culture that can transform those powerful ideas into reality.

Chapter 1

Quo Vadis: Why Organizations Are Losing Their Way

Whom the gods would destroy, they first grant forty years of business success.

Peter F. Drucker

There Will Always Be a Sears, IBM, and General Motors . . . ?

The unthinkable is happening distressingly more often in business these days. More and more companies are facing difficulties and even crises of survival that go far beyond the usual ups and downs of the economic cycle. Something more basic is now going on, something that is causing fundamental subterranean changes in markets, competitive sectors, and even national economies. The well-known ways don't always work anymore.

There seems to be a growing crisis of confidence in the business world, and it's affecting all of the developed countries. The shock waves are being felt most intensely by the United States, the biggest of all mercantile economies, but they are spreading to affect all modern economies. Even the oldest,

1

most revered, and traditionally most successful American firms are facing unprecedented identity crises. A surprising number of firms that were once a sure bet in just about any stock portfolio are now in serious trouble or in disrepute.

Chief executives are falling like bowling pins. Could anyone have predicted in 1983 that by 1993 the chief executive officer of IBM would be forced out of office as a result of a decline in the company's market and financial performance? John Akers, a career executive and one of the quintessential American corporate leaders, found himself in the saddle of a horse that was going in the wrong direction. As the market for IBM's core business—mainframe computers—softened, as prices in its secondary personal computer market kept falling, and as most of its other lines of business weakened as well, IBM seemed to be a company without a strategy or a plan. And Akers was a man without a job.

Similarly, General Motors had for decades enjoyed the reputation as one of the all-time corporate stalwarts. But years of inertia put GM as well as the other two of the "big three" American automakers behind the power curve. The agonizing slowness with which they responded to the Japanese "quality revolution," a proliferation of products from other foreign carmakers, and a significant recession all conspired to create losses in the billions of dollars. The company's board of directors perceived Chairman John Stempel and his team as having no real strategy for facing the situation, and he was handed his walking papers.

Who would believe that Sears, the retailing giant that for years was a symbol of virtually all that was American, could fall from the number-one market position to number three, behind upstarts Wal-Mart and K-Mart? Under a geriatric, caretaker leadership, the company had become so fossilized that it lost its franchise with the American household. It had to sell off a batch of unrelated businesses that it couldn't manage effectively. The final indignity was the closing of its mail-order catalog operation, which for generations had been a defining symbol of Americana. After the shock, Sears's management had to embark on an agonizing examination of the company's basic premise for its business operation.

These crises were not accidents of nature, quirks of the marketplace, or flukes. The list goes on. None other than

Kodak Corporation, the lifelong memory-maker of American families through vacations, birthday parties, graduations, weddings, and countless other personal experiences, started having trouble with its own business picture. The phenomenal popularity of video cameras and other electronic media threatened the market for conventional film products. Kodak faced the need to redefine itself as an *imaging products* company, no longer a photographic products company. Its board of directors decided CEO Kay Whitmore wasn't up to the task and arranged for his departure.

The list of sacrificial CEOs doesn't end there. James Robinson was forced out of American Express Corporation. Ken Olsen, a legend in the computer industry, was forced out of his position as CEO of Digital Electronics Corporation. In the late 1980s the legendary Steven Jobs, one of the founding eggheads of Apple Computer, was forced out of his position as chairman of the company as his handpicked CEO, John Sculley—formerly of Pepsi—brought in professional management approaches that displaced much of the "blue jeans" culture Jobs and his soulmates had created.

It's easy for us as bystanders and onlookers to pontificate about these highly visible examples, and to knowingly sum up the "reasons" for their crises. It's easy to declare the CEOs incompetent, misguided, or simply not up to the task of redefining their firms. But that would be missing an essential point, as well as unfair. These people, for the most part, were unusually intelligent, educated, experienced, and knowledgeable about their industries. None of them were bumblers. In some cases, boards of directors have sacrificed competent executives for "box office" effect, determined to show that they were doing their own duties properly.

But the real point of this discussion is the basic challenge of redefinition itself. If it can happen to IBM, Sears, General Motors, Kodak, American Express, Digital Equipment Corporation, and others, then it can happen to any company. Nobody is safely and permanently successful in the new business era. J. W. "Bill" Marriott, who founded the Marriott Corporation in 1927, starting with a chain of A&W Root Beer shops, declared: "Success is never final." He believed that it's harder to stay at the top than it is to get there.

The truth is that most or all of the organizations so far

mentioned would probably have come to their crises in one way or another, regardless of the person in charge at the time. The world changed. Markets changed. Customers changed. Technology changed. And the companies, originally defined to cope with a world that now no longer exists, were caught in the crosscurrents of these changes.

IBM laid off employees for the first time in its seventy-year history—over 100,000 of them. General Motors put over 50,000 of its people out of jobs. Procter and Gamble eliminated some 13,000 jobs and closed nearly 20 percent of its worldwide manufacturing capacity. General Dynamics jettisoned over 10,000 workers, victims of the relatively sudden end of the Cold War between the United States and the Soviet Union. Employees and managers of many other aerospace and military-goods firms suffered the same fate.

Airline companies in the United States racked up losses in a period of about five years that exceeded all their collective profits since the Wright brothers' first takeoff at Kitty Hawk in 1903. For many companies, falling revenues during the recession only masked more serious problems of business logic and changing economic infrastructure. Journalists dutifully blamed the job cuts on the recession of 1988–1992, but many of the problems were actually basic structural effects. Many of the reductions would have been inevitable, recession or not. Most of those jobs will never return.

General Motors will probably never be as large as it was at its peak, when it employed some 800,000 people. It must restructure itself for a new world. Mass markets are fast breaking up into minimarkets, and many megacorporations will likely fraction themselves into minicorporations. It makes just as much sense for GM to spin off smaller, targeted operations that can confront the competitive forces that are rapidly differentiating themselves in the transportation market. Maybe IBM would work better as a constellation of smaller, more focused, and more dynamic enterprises.

There is a conventional wisdom often expressed by observers of new, rapidly expanding technology markets. The pundits sagely predict that "In a few years, there will only be three to five big players left. All the small fish will either disappear or get swallowed up." The evidence for this view of the future is less and less compelling. The game is no longer won or lost based on who has the deepest pockets or access to the most capital. It is more and more being played on the basis of who can deploy resources most effectively to create customer value and competitive advantage. Big is no longer better. In some cases, it may not even be good.

While the three biggest airlines in the world, United, American, and Delta, struggle to stay above the red ink, small-niche player Southwest Airlines continues to post a respectable profit. While the major lines cut each other to pieces in suicidal fare wars, giving back their prior-year profits to their customers, Southwest sticks to a successful formula that gives it a commanding position in local short-haul markets.

Who made the personal computer a product so successful that it became a sociotechnical phenomenon in its own right? Certainly not IBM, the biggest and most powerful of all firms in the "computer market," defined previously as the mainframe business. It was a small company that was literally jump-started from a garage operation by two California whiz kids, Steve Jobs and Steve Wozniak. Why didn't Big Blue, the company traditionally considered synonymous with computers, introduce the PC? Why did IBM take so long to enter the market, and with such mediocre products? Why did it not take the PC phenomenon seriously for at least five years, as the industry was being created by small upstart companies?

But remember that success is never final. Why did Apple Computer, Compaq, and other major PC marketers laugh at the idea of selling computers by mail? While they jeered at the very notion that consumers would be willing to buy a box of parts with no added-value "service" provided by the retail store, consumers realized they weren't getting any service from retailers to speak of, and they responded to Michael Dell's market message. The computer became a generic product, and Dell Computers rapidly grew to a billion-dollar operation selling custom-assembled computers by mail. It took IBM years to finally open a direct-marketing computer operation. Somewhere around 1990, people stopped referring to PCs as "IBM-compatible" and just started calling them PCs. IBM had lost its putative franchise as the computer seller of choice.

This is not to say that size doesn't matter, only that

megasize may not be the answer. It isn't likely we'll see a commercial world of small mom-and-pop businesses with very few megafirms left. And anybody who underestimates a firm like IBM, which at any one time sits atop cash assets in the neighborhood of $5 billion, is making a serious mistake. General Motors will almost surely sustain its profitability over the long term, as will most other giants that are now struggling.

But nothing rises to the sky. Growth begets its own problems and eventually can pave the way for its own downfall. What is needed in the new era of business is a better answer to the question "Why?" as well as good answers to the question "How?" We're no longer talking about just the megacorporations of the world. We're talking about all business enterprises, from the greatest to the smallest. More and more organizations, even noncommercial ones like government agencies, associations, trade groups, and nonprofit enterprises, are facing fundamental questions of destiny. They are facing the need to redefine themselves, to rethink what they are doing in the most basic ways.

Shock Waves and Shock Wave Riders

In 1964 the town of Hilo, on the island of Hawaii, was almost entirely destroyed by a giant tidal wave, more accurately characterized by scientists as a *tsunami.* An incredible wall of water traveled for hundreds of miles at high speed from its origins in the Pacific Ocean, slamming into the shore community with astonishing force. These amazing killer waves are thought by scientists to originate in rare but powerful seismic events that occur under the surface of the ocean, transferring tremendous energy through the sea above them and erupting into surface waves of great speed and force. All of the Hawaiian Islands now have tsunami warning systems, but there is little anyone can do about them except to use the few precious hours of reaction time to relocate to higher ground.

It's becoming clear that there are also figurative waves, much like tsunami waves, erupting in various dimensions of national and international life. These economic, technological, social, and political *shock waves* can have profound effects on the business environment, changing the threats and opportunities facing the firms trying to operate in that environment, and changing the options and resources at their disposal for surviving. Part of defining or redefining the destiny of an enterprise must be understanding the shock waves in its environment and deciding what they mean to the business.

We can make good use of this shock wave metaphor to better understand the environment the enterprise must deal with. For this purpose we can define a shock wave as:

> An irreversible trend or movement powerful enough to restructure the basic realities of doing business.

A shock wave typically originates, much like a tsunami, in a triggering event or change that may at first be subterranean. That is, the event may not be detected until the shock wave it creates signals its existence by implication. Defining or redefining the concept of the business must now involve recognizing and adapting to the shock waves we can see, and possibly even predicting the arrival of shock waves our logic or intuition tells us must surely come.

According to business journalist, author, and speaker Ron Zemke, the successful leaders of the future will have to be *shock wave riders*, able to see the long waves coming and able to position their figurative surfboards above those waves. The more skillful of them will actually benefit from the rising waves, capitalizing on their movement and the restructuring they cause. Those who fail to see the waves coming, or who fail to react appropriately or quickly enough, may suffer serious losses in competitive position and in some cases may not even survive.

What are some of the shock waves we already know about that are affecting and will affect businesses around the world? At least six of them come to mind as nearly universal in their effect:

1. *The Japanese "quality miracle."* Reacting to a very negative image of Japan following World War II as the world's supplier of cheap junk products, Japanese industrial leaders undertook

a virtual revolution in attitudes, spirit, and work methods that created a base of skills and technology which enabled them to compete in almost any product arena they chose. The dominance of American and European firms in consumer electronics, cameras, automobiles, and even heavy equipment steadily gave way to the onslaught of lower-priced Japanese products that were often superior in quality as well.

In many cases Japanese products became the standards for comparison rather than the imitators. A number of Western firms virtually abandoned various products and product lines, conceding that they couldn't compete successfully with the Japanese. Coupled with extremely restrictive import practices, both formal and informal, that protected home markets from foreign competition, Japanese industry piled up enormous trade surpluses with the United States and with most other Western countries.

This shock wave changed the rules for doing business: Product quality became paramount, manufacturing technology had to improve vastly to meet aggressive Japanese pricing strategies, and many Western companies suddenly developed quality-image problems as second-rate suppliers. Xerox Corporation, for example, the pioneer and leader in the field of photocopying machines, suddenly discovered that the Japanese had a product that worked better, and which they could sell at a retail price lower than Xerox's base manufacturing cost. This was a wake-up call of unprecedented magnitude for Western businesses, but many of them took an ungodly long time in rousing themselves.

2. *The microelectronic revolution.* Triggered by the development of the digital "computer on a chip" in the early 1970s, and continuing through a series of astonishing advances in design and manufacturing technology, a whole new business subculture of high-tech firms began marketing commercial products ranging all the way from digital watches to electronic heart pacemakers. The Apple II computer, developed and marketed by Steve Jobs and Steve Wozniak, although not commercially impressive over the longer run, made the idea of the personal computer plausible. The idea that a small machine on one's desk could actually do as much as or more than the

traditional huge mainframe computer was a revolution in thinking.

With the rise of the digital way of doing things, and the phenomenal strides in microchip capability at the same time prices were being drastically reduced, the whole world began going digital. Personal computers proliferated throughout business organizations, multiplying the knowledge-processing capability of workers manyfold, and opening up ways of working not previously available. This trend led to an enormous demand for software and computer-related products.

This shock wave restructured business realities by making the impossible possible. The relentless advances in chip technology made digital products more familiar and more plausible, with the result that computers became relatively cheap commodities rather than exotic technoproducts. Digital clocks and watches, digital telephone answering machines, fax machines, and a host of other microelectronic products created whole new markets overnight and destroyed others. The hand-cranked desk calculator used by merchants became a museum relic. The traditional analog watch nearly disappeared from the scene as digital watches came in, only to reemerge as a style option with battery-powered microelectronic workings in place of the centuries-old mechanical mainsprings and escapements. By the time they staged a comeback with the Swatch product, Swiss watchmakers had learned a brutal lesson about not seeing shock waves coming. Incidentally, Swiss engineers had developed prototype versions of digital watches well before the Japanese, but industry leaders refused to believe the product had a future.

3. *The oil-price shock.* The sudden rise in oil prices beginning about 1972—brought about largely by the ability of the OPEC cartel of Middle Eastern oil-producing countries to ration their production, along with structural changes in the world petroleum market—caused all kinds of restructuring in various industries. Companies in energy-intensive industries had to find ways to reduce consumption radically. The rise in gasoline prices signaled the death knell for the oversized American cars, known in some countries as the "Yank tanks." It triggered a relentless technological march toward fuel efficiency. In many

ways, it gave the Japanese carmakers a head start in penetrating American markets, because Detroit carmakers dawdled for several years before they finally began to take the new economics seriously.

Although Europeans and Asians had long been accustomed to high fuel prices, Americans were new to the fuel-shortage game. Gasoline rationing in the early 1970s made it clear to Americans that their country no longer called all the shots in the world economy.

The oil shock radically drove up the cost of air travel. It also created great confusion in the American oil industry over time, because the OPEC nations kept whipsawing their prices and shifting supply levels to keep American oil companies off balance. Just about the time when oil prices were so high as to make new drilling feasible in North America, the OPEC cartel would boost production and force prices lower to destroy the incentives. Americans moaned and complained about their dependence on foreign oil, but none of a succession of administrations in Washington ever succeeded in creating a viable national energy policy.

4. *The collapse of communism.* Perhaps the most amazing political and economic phenomenon of the post–World War II era, the caving in of communist regimes changed many things. It changed the character of military planning in NATO countries and the United States in particular. It created wild fantasies of new markets as formerly communist countries would surely hunger for Western-style consumer goods as well as basic industrial products. Many of those fantasies were slow to come true, but the basic premise seemed appealing.

The American defense industry shuddered immediately at the prospect of massive cuts in the national budget for weapons systems and all of the associated matériel. Aerospace firms scrambled to find ways to redeploy their heavy capital assets and find new markets for their technological expertise, again with less than outstanding success in the beginning. For example, AM General, in South Bend, Indiana, decided to market a civilian version of its "HumVee" super-jeep. But with prices ranging from $35,000 to $75,000, buyers stayed away in droves.

The imminent closure of military bases, not only in the

United States but in other parts of the world, posed wrenching economic problems for communities that had grown up around them, depending on them for jobs as well as demand for locally supplied goods and services.

In a way, the communist-collapse shock wave caused a restructuring which we might describe as an asset transfer from General Dynamics to McDonald's. While General Dynamics, Rockwell, Lockheed, and other aerospace giants were losing government contracts and laying off thousands of employees, McDonald's was opening up the biggest hamburger restaurant in the world, right smack in downtown Moscow.

5. *The rise of service economies.* All of the Western industrial nations, and America in particular, experienced the shift toward service economies, with fewer of their people deployed in manufacturing jobs. The rise of global and transnational corporations accelerated the emigration of labor-intensive industries outward toward third world countries with lower labor costs. At the same time, service industries such as health care, fast food, travel, leisure and hospitality, and entertainment grew rapidly.

The closing or consolidation of factories caused massive restructuring in the American workforce as well as those of other industrialized countries experiencing the same transformation. Even Japan, which in the postwar years attracted heavy industry with its low labor costs, began to lose its grip on industries such as steel making, garment making, and auto fabrication, as its standard of living rose and its labor costs could not match those of countries like Taiwan, Korea, the Philippines, Indonesia, China, and others.

Countries like America tended to hold on to the high-value-added production processes that required exotic technology or more highly skilled workers. Japan has been experiencing much the same shift and revision of its workforce needs.

6. *The age wave.* The so-called age wave experienced by America, and to some extent most other highly industrialized countries, saw a decline in birth rates during the war combined with a surge in birth rates following the war and an increase in life expectancy. This created a disproportionate bump in the population curve, which is currently passing through the range

from about age 35 through age 50. The American postwar baby boom and related demographic phenomena in other countries caused a radical restructuring of demand for consumer products and a shift in product preferences.

As one random example of many restructuring effects, this aging population cohort has made golf a more preferred recreational activity. As people pass through their forties, they become somewhat less athletic and more sedentary, shifting their preferences from pastimes like tennis toward milder forms of exertion like golf. Many of these impacts of the population shift are so demographically predictable that industries rise and fall with the age wave. In most of the developed countries, the over-sixty population is steadily increasing, while the proportion of infants and children is decreasing. This is exactly the reverse of the situation in most developing countries, which are still turning out new citizens faster than they are retiring the older ones. The advanced countries will be facing very different problems and opportunities than the developing countries.

In addition to these global mega–shock waves, there have been various local shock waves causing upheaval and restructuring in specific industries. Almost every major industry or economic sector has one or more shock waves that are restructuring its business realities. In health care, for instance, major changes in the ways American government agencies pay for treatments have restructured business practices and changed the supply-and-demand equation. Further shocks here are virtually certain. Changes in tax laws have restructured real estate markets considerably. In financial services, advances in communication technology have linked various stock exchanges and commodities markets into a quasi-global market that reacts ever more quickly to global economic developments.

Shock waves come in all sizes as well as all shapes. Some smaller shock waves, happening in certain industries, could more realistically be considered simple trends. They are changes we need to understand and to monitor, but they may not necessarily be powerful enough to restructure basic business realities, which is our working definition of a shock wave.

In any case, in establishing the basic meaning and direction for the business, its leaders must face up to the known shock waves, concentrate on exploiting the various important trends, and be alert to manage critical events that could hand the enterprise great opportunities to strengthen its position in its business environment.

Road Map to Nowhere: The Price of Confusion

It is said that revolutions throw people into three different roles, or modes of performance: those who lead the revolution, those who follow it, and those who sleep through it. These days, the sleepers are in real trouble: What you don't know can kill you.

The time to start thinking about the meaning and direction of the business is not when things start going to hell but well in advance of the shock wave. Any business whose leaders do not have a clear sense of where the environment is going and what kind of a future the business must prepare for may be risking its actual survival.

An incident from my military training many years ago often comes to mind in any discussion of strategy and business direction. As young army officers, we were taken out into the woods, divided up into teams of ten, and given various tactical problems to solve. On one particular dark night, my team had the mission of ambushing a small force of "enemy" soldiers (actually training officers playing the part) encamped at the edge of a clearing. We had spent a long time creeping as quietly as we could until we were within about fifty meters of the camp. The training policy was to rotate the command of the units on a regular basis, so one of our number had been appointed leader of this hit squad.

As we stopped within sight of the enemy campfire, our leader seemed hesitant and confused and to have run out of plans. As we lay on our bellies behind a grassy ridge, we pressed him, in very intense whispers, for his course of action. When he finally blurted out the whispered command "Advance until fired upon!" and the instruction had passed along the line, he nearly had a mutiny on his hands. "Advance until fired upon! What kind of a !#@&&$#! strategy is that?!" we demanded. No one was willing to follow him on the basis of such a tenuous proposition. It took us about fifteen minutes to negotiate an approach to the attack, during which time I'm certain the "enemy" soldiers must have heard our buzzing and shuffling about. They could have easily mounted a counter-offensive if they chose to.

The "default" strategy for many businesses seems to be "advance until fired upon." In other words, there is no strategy except to keep moving in the current direction and hope nothing bad happens. The leaders of most enterprises seldom think the unthinkable. In fact, many of them fail even to think the thinkable.

Small companies in particular tend to run on intuition. The meaning and direction may be reasonably clear to the leaders, who translate it into day-to-day business decisions for everybody else. But as firms grow larger and more successful, and their worlds become ever more complex, they often run into a "fog phase," in which things don't seem so clear any-more. The chief executive is distressed to hear people saying things that indicate they don't understand or don't accept the key priorities of the business. Factionalism arises, and people draw battle lines. The "one happy family" concept gives way to a collection of clans, who may not perceive themselves as having any one common cause that unites them.

Of course, this is even more likely to happen in larger organizations, if only because size itself increases diversity, disparity, ambiguity, confusion, and conflict. The chief execu-tive may feel very strongly that the meaning and direction of the business are clear and compelling. But if the other execu-tives, tactical leaders, and rank-and-file employees can't artic-ulate it in some valid way, then for all practical purposes there isn't one.

Even worse, there may be conflicting views in the minds of the various executives about the direction. The lack of a single concept doesn't mean there are no concepts. Worse yet, the chief may not realize there are disparities or may not grasp the profound differences in worldview that are operating in the minds of the others. It is not at all uncommon for one key executive to have his or her own private view of the critical success parameters of the business while the CEO is pursuing another view. These differences of worldview may appear in the form of executive politics and divisional factionalism, but in reality those are often the symptoms that signal the underlying confusion.

This intellectual divisiveness can be extremely limiting and even destructive for the enterprise, even without the effects of scattered energies, political game playing, and internal conflict that it tends to cause. We can take it as a maxim that:

> If the organization is at war with itself, it can never be very effective on the battlefield of business.

Intellectual factionalism inevitably begets operational factionalism. If the senior leaders do not see a common vision and do not speak with a common voice, how can the tactical leaders at other levels do so? How can they achieve clarity of purpose for their own teams when none is available to them?

Therefore, we can also take it as a maxim that:

> Clarity of meaning and direction throughout the organization can never be any greater than it is at the top.

Indeed, it will almost always be less. Relatively few executives have so skillfully deployed their strategy throughout the organization that the typical working person fully understands where the enterprise is going and what part he or she is expected to play in its success. The normal state of affairs is for the worker or unit-level leader to have less clarity in his or her mind than the CEO has. In too many cases, there is much less. Often, in fact, the CEO may not really care whether the "wage mules," as one executive calls them, understand the big picture.

It is heartbreaking to see what happens in the organization when a chief executive seems to start each day with a clean sheet of paper. False starts, redirections, commitments that come unstuck, and capricious ad hoc decision making keep everyone off balance. Senior executives can't possibly interpret direction for their tactical leaders in any meaningful way. And the further down the organizational maze one goes, the fuzzier and more indistinct becomes the picture of what the enterprise stands for and what people can hope to commit their energies to.

A few executives even seem to take a perverse pride in not declaring a course of action that makes them predictable. From his or her own selfish perspective, such a person may feel safer for not having locked into a strategy or plan that might turn out to be wrong or ill conceived. One CEO I knew even commented, "I like to stir things up every now and then, just to show them who owns the spoon." Would-be leaders like this seldom have any grasp of the extent to which they have crippled their organizations and constrained the effectiveness of the brainpower at their disposal.

Contrast this amoebic pattern of management with that of organizations in which people do know where they are going. World leaders such as Disney, Federal Express, Toyota, Matsushita Electric, Sweden's Volvo, Swiss-and-Swedish ASEA Brown-Boveri, Xerox, Wal-Mart, Nordstrom Department Stores, France's Club Méditerranée, and Switzerland's Nestlé are all strong-culture enterprises whose people understand what the model for excellence is and know what to do to make it work. None of them is perfect, and none is immune from blunders and setbacks, but they all start with the significant advantage of knowing who they are and what value they must create in order to succeed.

Far too many executives, in charge of all sorts of organizations in all sorts of industries, fail to grasp the value and the difficulty of effective *strategy deployment*, although there is no shortage of historical examples that show how it empowers people in remarkable ways. Dr. Charles Garfield, a noted speaker and the author of *Peak Performers*, has studied the effect of what he calls "mission psychology." During his work as a computer scientist in the U.S. space program during the years of Apollo 11, he was struck by the intense fervor with which people worked toward the one superordinate goal they all understood.[1]

In 1960, President John F. Kennedy had declared the goal, simply and unequivocally:

> I believe that this nation should commit itself to achieving the goal, before this decade is out, of landing a man on the moon and returning him safely to Earth.[2]

That declaration became the manifesto, the organizing principle that gave meaning and direction not only to the space program but to the professional lives of many creative technical people in government and in the aerospace industry.

Says Garfield, "I had never seen such a group of people work with such absolute focus and fervor as those people, who saw it as their own personal *mission* to send astronauts to the moon. They worked incredibly long hours, under intense pressure, and they loved it. They had something that added meaning and value to their own lives, and they gave 200 percent to make it come true."[3]

Believe it or not, there are business organizations in which people work that same way. There are firms in which people know what counts, and they personally own the success premise of the enterprise. They are invariably firms whose leaders have, in the words of University of Southern California professor Warren Bennis, "created a vision for success, and learned how to enroll others in that vision."

Vision, Illusion, or Hallucination?

But to enlist the kind of energy that Garfield, Bennis, and other leadership experts talk about requires actually *having* a vision, a meaning, and a direction, one that is not only clear but valid and compelling. While many enterprises have no clear statement of direction at all, many others are self-deluded, believing they do. There is direction, and then there is *direction*. Too many firms have trivial, meaningless "mission statements" and other supposedly inspiring documents that say nothing. Too many executives and executive teams settle for "puff" journalism in place of critical thinking.

With regard to the Apollo program, suppose Kennedy had phrased the mission differently? Suppose he had said "We are going to conquer space," or "We are going to beat the Russians in the space race," or "We are going to lead the world in space technology"? Would it have had the same compelling meaning as "landing a man on the moon" "before this decade is out"?

Consider the following mission statement of a real but unidentified company:

Our Mission Statement

[ABC] aims to provide superior value and service to its customers.

How effective is this statement? Can you tell what kind of a business it represents? Can you even identify the industry? Can you glean from it a sense of competitive focus, a value premise for its customers, or any form of market differentiation? This statement appeared on one side of a small laminated wallet card given to me by an executive at a cocktail party. The other side of the card said:

Service Strategy

We will deliver superior value and service to our customers by:

- having the authority to make decisions.
- supporting each other with technology and training.
- supportive leadership.
- recognizing and rewarding superior service.

I don't know how long it took to develop that statement. I believe it's the mission statement of a shipping firm.

Try another, the mission statement of a railway company:

Mission

[XYZ] people will excel in meeting customer needs by providing safe, competitive, and efficient transport services.

Can you identify the customer from this mission statement? Do you know what the company is doing for the customer? Do you know how it intends to win and keep the customer's business? Would you as an employee of this firm know how to channel your energies to help your company succeed?

Too many corporate statements of purpose are like these: vague, bland, uninspiring, and virtually without meaning. As we progress in this book through the thinking process associated with creating meaning and direction and deploying that meaning throughout the organization, we will need to consider some criteria for doing so effectively. In reading what follows, you will find it necessary to search your own mind for the criteria that make sense to you and compare them to the criteria I will offer. We may not always agree. What might be an effective mission statement to you might not pass my test, and vice versa. We do not have to agree completely, but the issue of the effectiveness of the corporate "constitution" is a critical one that deserves careful thought.

We will develop some criteria for testing various statements of meaning and direction for validity, power, and impact. Please bear in mind throughout the discussion that there is no one universal criterion, no universal form or format, and no one way of writing such statements that is "correct." The ultimate test of any statement of vision, mission, values, philosophy, or business direction is its effectiveness in mobilizing people to a common purpose. However, I do advocate fairly strongly certain approaches that I believe are more effective than most others.

I will try to allow as much latitude for alternative ways of looking at the problem, but I will accept responsibility for putting forth a fairly definite view about how to do it. Chapter

9 deals in depth with the process of formulating various statements of purpose for your enterprise.

The Northbound Train: The Power of a Common Cause

One of the most useful business metaphors I've come across is
the idea of "the northbound train" as an image that conveys
an unwavering commitment to a particular direction. The person who first mentioned it to me attributed it to a management
consultant and educator named Harold Hooke, a man I've
never met. I don't know whether Hooke invented it or where
he got it, but it's too bad people don't always get the credit for
the ideas they create. In any case, I've always liked the sense
of imperative conveyed by the term.

Think about the implications of the northbound train:
purpose and direction. No vision statement or mission statement can ever make much sense unless it originates in some
valid concept about what it takes to succeed. It is not a platitude. It is not a slogan. It is not an exercise in journalism; it is
an exercise in careful, clear, creative, disciplined, and mature
thought. It provides a *critical success premise* that leaders can
understand, commit to, and dramatize to others.

The idea of a moving train also conveys a strong sense of
momentum, of unstoppable, implacable movement in an un-
ambiguous direction. I've seen many executives adopt the
metaphor in communicating their determination to their leadership team. "This," they will say, "is our northbound train.
This is the direction we have chosen, and no other. If you don't
feel you want to go north, there are other trains you can ride.
But this particular train is going north, and I expect anyone
who rides it to commit his or her energies fully to the journey."

> The Northbound Train:
> The fundamental driving idea of the business,
> before which all resistance crumbles.

But even if the metaphor is useful, the questions arise,
"How do we figure out what our particular northbound train

is? We aren't Federal Express, or Singapore Airlines, or Philips, or Siemens, or Club Med. We're who we are, so how do we transform the concept of who we are into a compelling north-bound train idea of our own?"

This is the challenge we will take up throughout this book. These questions do not have simple, one-liner answers. The answers come about through a careful process of creative thinking and logical reasoning that must be unique to each individual enterprise. Nevertheless, the process does have certain fundamental features that make it relevant to almost all strategy challenges. We will develop the process in stages and see how it can apply to organizations of many kinds and in many situations.

Notes

1. Charles Garfield, *Peak Performers: The New Heroes of American Business* (New York: William Morrow, 1986).
2. Judie Mills, *John F. Kennedy* (New York: Franklin Watts, 1988), p. 210.
3. Garfield, *Peak Performers*.

Chapter 2

Beyond Executive Management: The Call for Leadership

Some men see things that are, and ask "Why?"
I see things that never were, and ask "Why not?"

Robert Kennedy

The Crisis of Meaning

In many ways the crisis in business today is a crisis of meaning. People aren't sure of themselves because they no longer understand the why behind the what. They no longer have the sense that things are well defined and that hard work will lead to success. More and more people have feelings of doubt and uncertainty about the future of their organizations, and consequently about their own careers and futures. More and more organizations and their people are in a crisis of meaning.

In many ways also the crisis of meaning for business organizations mirrors a crisis of meaning for nations, a crisis confronting people in many countries. Visit any of the major developed countries in the world and chances are you'll see an unprecedented preoccupation with questions of national purpose, cultural values, and priorities. Leaders of these nations are beset on all sides by contradictory pressures, extremist agendas, and demands for solutions. They are asking themselves: Who are we as a nation? What do we stand for? and, What should our focus and our priorities be now?

And at a personal level, more and more people seem to be experiencing a parallel or derivative sense of uncertainty. Social and moral values are under debate. Social activism is on the rise; some issues are so divisive as to create intense animosity and even violence. Many people seem focused more on what divides them than on what they have in common. There is a profound need for a sense of common purpose, a commitment to a common cause.

Those who would aspire to leadership roles in this new environment must not underestimate the depth of this human need for meaning. It is a most fundamental human craving, an appetite that will not go away. In his book *Man's Search for Meaning*, psychologist Victor Frankl expresses the view that all human beings need a defining purpose for their lives, something to believe in, something to hope for, something to strive for. Those who lose it or never acquire it become dysfunctional at best and criminally maladjusted at worst.[1]

Frankl describes his experiences in the Nazi concentration camps during the Second World War, in which he saw prisoners who he believed simply gave up and decided to die. Living under the most harsh and brutal conditions imaginable, those who had no higher purpose in life to cling to could not hold up under the stress. Those who, like himself, believed they would eventually return to something better after the camp experience was over were usually able to survive, at least psychologically. For some people it was a religious belief. For others, it was a meaningful role in helping other people. In Frankl's case, it was the unshakable belief that he would be reunited with his wife and children after the war was over.

Indeed, Frankl was so convinced of the central role of meaning in human life that, after he regained his freedom and returned to work, he made that concept the driving idea behind his psychotherapy practice. He even named his newly created specialty *logotherapy*, after the Greek word *logos*, which equates to the concept of "meaning." A *logotype*, or *logo*, is a graphic symbol used by an enterprise to communicate its identity to others. Used in marketing and advertising, logos can be very effective. The best leaders use figurative logos in communicating meaning within the enterprise itself, as well as with the external world.

We need a kind of logotherapy for organizations and the people living in them today. Perhaps it becomes a kind of *logoleadership,* or leadership through meaning. We can no longer rely on the forces of our environment to supply the meaning for what we do in business. Two or three decades ago, the business environment was much more stable, slow-changing, and therefore more predictable than it is now. Chief executives mostly knew what to do, and people had much of their meaning defined for them by the flow of events around them. The old imperatives were: Work hard, keep focused on doing the right things, do better each year, and grow incrementally.

The new imperatives are: Rethink the basics, adapt to new ways of doing business, reinvent processes, and let go of the past. In the midst of this kind of ever changing reality, it's no wonder that people hunger for stability, meaning, and truth in their lives. We human beings cannot function indefinitely in a state of alarm and confusion. If only for our own neurotic self-preservation, we will seek order and predictability in our lives, even if we have to create it artificially. People need meaning for what they do, and many will follow dictators, demagogues, and even maniacs to get it.

But this crisis of meaning, at least in business, is as much an opportunity as a problem. Those leaders who can offer their people a valid, meaningful success proposition, and help the people understand its value for them and the contribution they can make to it, have the best chance of mobilizing their energies and channeling their commitment toward worthwhile goals.

This, more than anything else, is the challenge for today's executives: to create meaning. It is not always easy, but those who can do it skillfully are more likely to be able to steer their organizations through difficult times.

We are coming to a point in business thinking where even the concept of management is suspect, and the basic term itself is falling into disrepute. *Management,* in its traditional connotation, has always implied the control of the many by the few.

It has signaled an autocratic, systematic, and intellectual thought process, not a human, dynamic, and personal one. Traditional B-school thinking has always viewed the manager as managing the organization, as if it were some kind of apparatus to be manipulated.

Dr. Warren Bennis, professor at the University of Southern California, asserts that today's employee is overmanaged and underled. "We have too much management in our organizations today, and not enough leadership." As we move ahead into ever more turbulent times and face ever more complex and challenging problems, there will be a shift of emphasis in management thinking. We must leave behind the traditional preoccupation with the organizational structure and its processes and move toward a much more diversified thinking process that focuses on the creation of value, mobilizes collective intelligence, and projects a compelling concept of the meaning of the enterprise. And we have to learn how to enable the people of the enterprise to create unprecedented levels of value for the customer, the organization, and themselves.

The Hand at the Helm

Just as the need for meaning has never been greater in the business world than now, so has the need for strong leadership never been greater. It is no longer enough for executives to merely preside over their organizations; they must lead and guide them. And the kind of leadership now called for is also different from that of the past. Enterprises need high-powered thinkers at the helm now, people with strong conceptual and visionary skills. A person who can exhort people, prod them, and move them to do big things will not be successful if he or she can't figure out what the right big things are. The complex changes, issues, and problems confronting businesses now demand a high level of *visionary leadership*.

Second, the new pattern of leadership must be an *enabling* pattern, not a commanding one. A leader might be quite impressive in his or her ability to command respect and deference, give orders, and see that they are carried out. But the way to release and mobilize the human energy in today's complex organizations is by empowering people with ideas and information, not telling them what to do. This calls for *service leadership,* not command leadership.

And third, today's executive must focus unwaveringly on the critical success factor in business, namely, *customer value.* This requires personally talking to and learning from customers, encouraging others throughout the organization to do the same, and making a relentless effort to translate the customers' advice into action.

Business leaders today must have both the visionary capacity and the service philosophy to create the northbound train idea, help people choose to ride on the train, and help them make sure it succeeds in its journey.

Certainly we need a new commitment to leadership at all levels of the organization, but for the present discussion we must acknowledge the special needs for executive leadership.

In the new world of rapid change, uncertainty, and customer-focused competition, the executive must take on four critical roles, or key dimensions of his or her contribution, as illustrated in Figure 2-1.

1. *A visionary* who creates meaning by crafting the vision, mission, and direction that define the focus of the enterprise;

Figure 2-1.   Executive leadership.

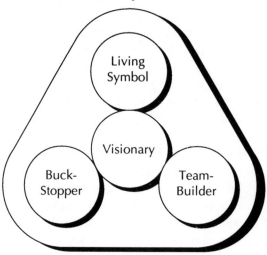

clarifying and distilling its northbound train concept; continuously evolving, elaborating, and interpreting this meaning for the people of the organization.

2. *A team-builder* who puts the right people in the right places for the top-level leadership team, welds them into a single-minded core of advocacy for the common cause, capitalizes on their individual strengths and resources, and continuously develops them as a team and as individual leaders who can serve the mandate required of them.

3. *A living symbol* who "walks the talk" in a highly visible way, demonstrating what is not necessarily a charismatic style of leadership but a constant and unrelenting pattern of reinforcing the northbound train concept at every opportunity. This involves simple, everyday actions and statements as well as ceremonial and celebratory actions that enable people to associate the leader inseparably with the success premise of the enterprise, so that seeing or hearing the leader automatically evokes in them powerful personal associations with the success concept. In this role the leader is figuratively a "human logo."

4. *A buck-stopper* who faces the difficult issues, discerns the truth of the challenges presented by the environment, and makes the tough decisions and dramatic changes that have to be made. This must, of course, involve open-minded listening and collaboration with the leadership team, but ultimately it is the chief executive who must face the music and manage the organization's response to critical issues.

These critical roles apply just as well to all of the executives in the leadership team as to the chief executive. Each of them must be a visionary, a team-builder, a living symbol, and a buck-stopper for his or her own enterprise within the enterprise. While we can allow for natural differences in personalities and personal styles of leadership, and not expect any one executive to be a psychological clone of the chief, nevertheless it is important that all top-level leaders face up to these four key roles. At lower levels of the organization, tactical leaders must focus more directly on carrying out the direction, in response to the kinds of leadership they receive from the top.

Think of these four roles in terms of the problems organizations tend to have when their executives fall short in filling them. An organization without strong leadership begins to disintegrate psychologically and even spiritually. Depending on the nature of its operations, it begins to malfunction, wasting energy, talent, and costly resources. To use a term borrowed from the systems analysis field, it experiences an increase in *entropy*, which is a measure of lost coherence, synergy, and internal energy efficiency. As entropy increases, the organization begins to fall apart.

In many ways, an organization with weak leadership tends to resemble a dysfunctional family, especially as time goes on and the leaders fail to meet its needs for meaning, direction, and focus. Just as children in parentless families squabble with one another, so do departments fall into political games and feuds. Just as the uproar of an alcoholic parent distorts and immobilizes family processes, so do executive rampages and palace wars create fear and self-defensive maneuvering among lower-level managers.

In a weakly led organization, the old addictions begin to resurface, with selfish, self-preserving behaviors displacing those of cooperation, generosity, camaraderie, and altruism. People turn away from the enterprise as a source for their personal meaning and satisfaction and turn inward toward their own self-interests. In advanced stages of dysfunctional leadership, there may even be an increase in dishonest, unethical behavior as people abandon any personal connections they may have had with the culture of the enterprise.

By contrast, consider the state of affairs when the chief executive and the members of the top team do indeed step up to the challenges of the four roles of visionary, team-builder, living symbol, and buck-stopper. They have a common cause in their minds, and they carry that message all through the organization. They function effectively as a team, and they expect leaders at all levels to be team-builders as well. They show people, by every word and deed, that the northbound train idea is the way to success, and they symbolize by their behavior the vision and the values behind it. And they show that they are willing and able to face the difficult problems that confront the enterprise as it unfolds toward its vision of success.

People in a well-led organization tend to leave behind their old dysfunctional patterns and move toward involvement, commitment, cooperation, and a sense of shared fate. They accept and act upon the reality of their interdependence. Although even the healthiest cultures have a normal level of "politics," in a well-led enterprise the force of the vision and direction override the day-to-day frictions and collisions. People look to their leaders for answers, and they look to the culture for at least some of their sense of psychological reward.

In the well-led organization there is a shared ethic of performance, a real desire to see the enterprise succeed, and a personal commitment to quality work. Whereas in the poorly led organization people tend to move away from or against one another and their leaders, in the well-led organization they tend to move with and toward them. They see their personal success as in some way connected to the success of the enterprise.

This, then, is the real strategic challenge. The power of the northbound train concept—the common cause—comes when the enterprise has a strong hand at the helm. Creating the northbound train concept and helping people live it is much more than an intellectual exercise. It requires the leaders of the enterprise to *deploy* the strategy, to build the infrastructure for implementing it, and to support the evolution of a healthy culture in which people succeed by committing their energies toward its success.

Service Leadership: To Lead Is to Serve

One of the Latin titles used to refer to the pope is *servus servorum*, which means "the servant of servants." This point of view suggests that anyone in a leadership role, whether it involves formal authority or not, must lead by enabling others, not by trying to drive them.

In today's world, leaders are being called upon to provide a new kind of leadership: *service leadership*. Gone are the days when a simple "command and control" pattern would work. The old military style of the "kick in the butt" has outlived its usefulness. It no longer fits with contemporary social values, and it is no longer very effective. People in complex working situations need and expect positive personal relationships with their leaders, relationships that help them focus their energies, work at their best, surpass their expectations of themselves, and feel a sense of satisfaction in what they've contributed.

What is service leadership? It is *the capacity to lead with a service focus:*

- Service to the customer
- Service to the organization
- Service to the employees—those who do the work in achieving the objectives

It means working with a spirit and a set of values that emphasize contributing something worthwhile. It means that the leader sees his or her role as enabling or helping others to accomplish something worthy, not just being in charge.

The service leader is willing to put empowerment above personal power; contribution above his or her own ego satisfaction; and the needs of the team above his or her own needs for credit and acclaim. Albert Schweitzer, the famous physician and humanitarian, said:

> There is no higher religion
> than serving others.

Management consultant and author Peter Block advances the case for *stewardship* as a defining motif of service leadership in the new age:

> Stewardship means to hold in trust the well-being of some larger entity—our organization, our community, the earth itself. This . . . calls for placing service ahead of control, to no longer expect leaders to be in charge and out in front. Service is central to stewardship.
>
> We serve when we build capability in others by supporting ownership and choice at every level. When we act to create compliance in others, we are choosing self-interest over service, no matter what

words we use to describe our actions. Service-givers who maintain dominance, aren't. Stewardship enables the use of power with grace.[2]

The attitudes of service leadership are very different from those traditionally inculcated into managers, particularly male managers. The "testosterone factor" typically conditions males to think in terms of authority, control, and compliance rather than in terms of ownership, empowerment, and enablement. It seems clear, however, that more and more managers, both male and female, are moving toward a broader and more versatile view of their roles and are finding it comfortable to think in terms of leading through service.

Scandinavian Airlines chief executive Jan Carlzon even goes so far as to talk about "management by love." In his view,

Most authoritarian organizations tend to manage by fear, at least in the sense of imposing rules and punishing those who violate them. I don't believe any organization can rise above the level of mediocrity by maintaining a culture of fear. When people know they are secure in their roles, that they have someone they can turn to for help and guidance, and that their leaders believe in them, they are much more likely to go beyond the bounds of the ordinary, take risks, and contribute more of their energies and talents to the success of the organization. I call this "management by love."[3]

Customer-Focused Leadership: The Service Triangle

In the book *Service America! Doing Business in the New Economy*, Ron Zemke and I presented the "service triangle," illustrated in Figure 2-2, which is a pictorial model showing the importance of aligning the organization's strategy, people, and systems around the needs of its customers.[4] For some time we've been using this diagram in countless discussions, presentations, and writings about the management of service businesses.

People in business who are trying to focus their organiza-

Figure 2-2. The service triangle.

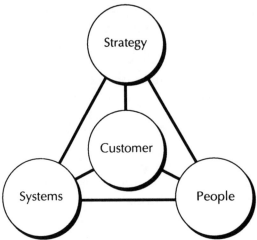

Source: © 1984 Karl Albrecht.

tions on "quality" are rapidly coming to the realization that *customer focus* must be the keystone of any effort to improve the organization's way of doing things. Isolated "quality programs" that measure and count things for the sake of measuring and counting are going out of style fast. This is why the *customer* goes at the center of the service triangle.

People in business are also beginning to realize that, to be successful, any organizationwide focus on quality must be driven by the basic demands of the business strategy. What do we want to be, and how do we intend to do business? If the vision, mission, core values, and key competitive concept of the organization are not clear, a quality program will suffer from lack of focus and direction. This is why the element of *strategy* goes at the top of the service triangle.

Another important lesson of the traditional manufacturing-style approach to quality is that the effort needs to have an element of heart if it is to succeed. Too many quality efforts begin as administrative, analytical, mechanistic, control-oriented, dehumanized, standards-based management attempts to "tighten up" the organization rather than loosen it up and empower the people to make their own individual quality commitments. This is why the doctrinaire, mechanistic TQM systems are ultimately doomed to failure. And this is why the *people* are fundamental to, not an obstacle in, the service triangle.

And the all-important *systems* go into the service triangle because they are the means for achieving the ends of superior customer value. All of the methods, procedures, equipment, machinery, tools, facilities, work processes, distribution systems, organizational structures, and information systems must work toward the ultimate purpose of creating or adding value—either for the external customers or for the internal customers who depend on support departments to achieve their missions.

The most important idea conveyed by the service triangle diagram is the *interplay* of these three organizational priorities and their impact on the customer's experience and perception of value. The strategy informs and enlightens the entire approach to the business and, consequently, the organization's attitudes about what value is and what it looks like to the customer. The people need to understand the customer and the business strategy, because ultimately they are the ones who must make the strategy a reality.

The design of the systems must also reflect the business strategy. How should we be organized to create and deliver the kinds of value the customer seeks? We need *customer-friendly systems* in all areas of the operation, whether the customers are external or internal.

And, of course, the design of the systems must support the people who have to deliver value. They need information, resources, and methods—the ways and means for creating an outstanding customer experience.

Finally, all three of the components of quality shown in Figure 2-2 impinge upon the customer's experience and lead him or her to form a judgment of the value we provide at the all-important moment of truth.

It is becoming obvious that the traditional distinction between so-called manufacturing organizations and service organizations is now obsolete and eventually may exist only in the minds of economists. In fact, both must deal with the same issues when it comes to quality. The only difference is in the relative balance of tangible value and intangible value respectively that they deliver.

As more and more executives come to understand the importance of a strategy-based, customer-value–centered approach to the success of their organizations, they are less confused by arbitrary distinctions such as "product," "quality," and "service." They begin to understand that the real issue is neither quality nor service, but *superior customer value*. And their job is to help the people of the organization create and deliver that value. The best way they can make their own contribution is by using their leadership abilities to align the strategy, people, and systems around the needs of their customers.

Mobilizing Intelligence: Collective Smartness or Dumbness?

The highest recorded IQ score, if I recall correctly, is somewhere in the neighborhood of 200. At that level, the scoring system tends to fall apart, and the actual number means less than the phenomenon itself.

Organizations have IQs, don't they? Did you ever wonder what the highest organizational IQ might be? Indeed, what is organizational IQ? How does an organization manifest its collective intelligence?

Some years ago, in a book titled *Brain Power*, I modestly drafted Albrecht's Law of Collective Dumbness:

> Intelligent people, when assembled into an organization, can sometimes do dumb things collectively.

Surely we all wonder from time to time whether it's possible for an organization to stop making the same mistakes over and over, and to use the collective knowledge, know-how, and wisdom it has. Yet we still see collective dumbness demonstrated repeatedly in everyday organizational life.

Case in point: I recently called a hospital in Kansas to inquire about the status of a patient, who was the husband of one of my associates, supposedly there for an emergency hip surgery. The person who answered the telephone transferred me to another person, who consulted her computer and informed me that there was no such person in the hospital. I asked her to double-check. She did and assured me they had no patient by that name. I was a bit confused, but I had to assume I was mistaken about his whereabouts.

That evening, I was able to reach my associate at the home of some friends and learned that her husband had been undergoing surgery in that hospital at the very moment I was being told he wasn't there. Is this a case of collective dumbness? And isn't it fairly typical of many organizations?

But there's an even worse version of collective dumbness, one that is much more profound and pernicious in its implications for organizational success or failure. It is the deliberate "dumbing down" of the workforce through traditional management techniques that have been accepted and glorified for four or five decades. While the Japanese are working hard at finding ways to leverage individual intelligence for collective good, many Western managers, academics, and management consultants are still working hard at figuring out how to *exclude* individual brain power from organizational processes. This is what Swedish managers refer to in American management practices as "the systematic stupification of the worker."

A worse case in point: In a recent article explaining the merits of a quality management technique called ISO 9000 certification, a consultant admonished his readers with something like the following:

> The ultimate test of the effectiveness of your documentation of the work processes is that, hypothetically, you could remove every one of the workers from the organization, bring in a completely new group of workers, and they would be able to operate the organization using the manuals you have created.

Have you ever seen an organization do such a thing? Can you think of a case in which it would be a desirable thing to do? Does it strike you that the author of the article has become so enamored of the process that he has lost sight of the ultimate organizational resource, which is its collective knowledge? He seems to believe that the competitive know-how of the organization resides in a huge shelfful of manuals rather than in the heads, hearts, hands, and instincts of the people of the organization. Does he propose to replace the executives and managers too, as a litmus test of the manuals? Does the test also apply to quality consultants?

In *Gulliver's Travels*, Lemuel Gulliver visited a strange land populated by a society of astronomers who spent their days engrossed in calculating the daily movements of the heavenly bodies. After having done this diligently for many generations, they had come to believe that if they didn't perform their calculations every day, the heavenly bodies would no longer move. I think we're seeing, in certain areas of management theory (and, unfortunately, in practice as well), a mind-set like that of Gulliver's astronomers.

Some of the most extreme practices of TQM, ISO 9000, and other "McManagement" approaches represent, in the words of one of my associates, "Frederick Taylor gone berserk."[5] Many jobs are so narrowly designed and overcontrolled that the employee cannot possibly deploy the wealth of practical knowledge, life experience, and common sense he or she brings to the job. Too many managers and quality practitioners fail to grasp that the real competitive know-how of an organization is implicit, in the collective understanding of its people, not explicit in a roomful of manuals.

Let's consider the prospect of organizational collective intelligence and see what kind of an attitude transplant is necessary on the part of the "astronomers." Let's suppose a typical organization or unit has 100 employees and that each of them has approximately the average IQ score of 100 points. Multiplying 100 IQ points by 100 people, we get a total of 10,000 IQ points. The critical question is, How many of these IQ points is our organization actually using? Bear in mind that we've already paid for them, whether we use them or not. When the employee shows up for work, we've already purchased his or her 100 or so IQ points, or at least we have an option on them. By the end of each day, we have either exercised the option or we've let it expire. That day will never come again, and the option on that day's IQ points is gone forever.

In his insightful book *Managing on the Edge,* Richard Pascale passes on a statement from a Japanese executive that is chilling in its directness and clarity. It is made by Konosuke Matsushita, founder of the huge firm Matsushita Electric, to his competitors and executive counterparts in the West:

> We are going to win and the industrial West is going to lose out; there's not much you can do about it because the reasons for your failure are within yourselves. Your firms are built on the Taylor model. Even worse, so are your heads. With your bosses doing the thinking while the workers wield the screwdrivers, you're convinced deep down that this is the right way to run a business. For you, the essence of management is getting the ideas out of the heads of the bosses and into the hands of the labor.
>
> We are beyond your mind-set. Business, we know, is now so complex and difficult, the survival of firms so hazardous in an environment increasingly unpredictable, competitive, and fraught with danger, that their continued existence depends on the day-to-day mobilization of every ounce of intelligence.[6]

While managers in America and other Western countries are busy figuring out how to standardize workers along with everything else in the organization, the Japanese are figuring out how to exercise the option on the IQ points. Just imagine the possibilities, if we could learn how to do it. Instead of starting with 10,000 IQ points and whittling them down to a few thousand or a few hundred by robotizing and standardizing the employees, suppose we could exercise the option on all 10,000 points. Suppose we could go even further and create synergy by inviting people to contribute their best ideas and inventions as well as their basic job knowledge. Suppose we could multiply the 10,000 IQ points a hundredfold. We would have a collective organizational IQ of one million.

In a business environment where cost-cutting, downsizing, and process redesign are coming to the point of diminishing returns, and yet profit margins are still being squeezed brutally, we must find new ways to make our organizations more effective and more competitive. Ultimately, even the most doctrinaire B-school thinker will have to face the fact that the only remaining variable resource we can really exploit is the gray matter.

As we move beyond intermediate concepts such as "quality," "service," and "management," we are coming to see more and more clearly that *value creation* is the higher premise for organizational effectiveness, and that collective intelligence is essential to achieving it.

It is now time to get down to cases and move forward with the task of really defining the northbound train. We need to find a means and an approach that will enable us to work through the challenging questions facing any business enterprise, and to develop a strategic success model. This is the goal and the process of the following chapters.

Notes

1. Victor Frankl, *Man's Search for Meaning: An Introduction to Logotherapy* (Boston: Beacon Press, 1992).
2. Peter Block, *Stewardship: Choosing Service Over Self-Interest* (San Francisco: Berrett-Koehler, 1992).
3. Speech given in Sao Paulo, Brazil.
4. Karl Albrecht and Ron Zemke, *Service America! Doing Business in the New Economy* (Homewood, Ill.: Irwin Professional Publishing, 1985).
5. See Frederick Taylor's brief book *The Principles of Scientific Management*, originally published in 1911 by Harper & Row, currently in print through W. W. Norton & Company, New York. Taylor is credited (especially by Peter Drucker) with leading the breakthrough in management thinking based on standardizing, encoding, and teaching efficient work practices. At the same time, he is vilified by others as having committed generations of managers to the mindless robotization of workers by eliminating originality and discretion in their work. Both camps are right to some extent.
6. Richard Pascale, *Managing on the Edge: How Successful Companies Use Conflict for Competitive Advantage* (New York: Simon and Schuster, 1990), p. 51.

Chapter 3

Learning the New Rules of the Game

And how am I to face the odds
Of man's bedevilment and God's?
I, a stranger and afraid
In a world I never made.

A. E. Housman, *Last Poems*

There is a great deal of hand-wringing these days about the turbulent business environment. Company fortunes rise and fall, products die or get eclipsed by others, technology tears traditional markets apart, strange alliances emerge among ex-competitors, bold business strategies fail and others succeed. A person who is inclined to be fearful or pessimistic will have no difficulty finding a reason.

And yet, all is not chaos. Some would have one believe that confusion is the order of the day, and that success in business is now just a crapshoot. But that worldview is not supported by the evidence. One just has to know how to read the signals and find the patterns that will be the new drivers of success in a new business environment. One has to learn the new rules of the game.

Did you ever have one of those strange dreams in which you showed up with your tennis racket to find your friends standing on a baseball diamond; and to make it worse, they were all carrying golf clubs? And the dream was all about trying to figure out what game you were supposed to be playing. It's a bit like that in business these days. The old playing field, the old players, the old equipment, and the old rules for scoring points don't always work now. It's becoming more and more important to rethink the game you're playing. Actually, the increasing change and upheaval in the business environment offer more possibilities than threats to those who are willing to take an innocent new look at how things work.

Finding the Driving Patterns

Although it isn't possible to reduce the rapidly changing business environment to a simple formula, we can still discern some basic realities that can get our feet back on the ground. We can find some patterns and a crude logic of sorts that help make sense of what's going on. What follows may seem slightly theoretical at times, but you will probably see, as the discussion progresses, how these patterns can affect your business.

In Chapter 1 we considered some of the shock waves that are tossing the boats of business organizations these days. Sharing the figurative ocean with those shock waves are various other "surface waves," that is, gentler but equally insistent movements that are also restructuring the business environment by changing the options open to enterprise leaders. By taking note of these surface waves and understanding the way they change options, we can begin to perceive a new order to things, even if it is a dynamic and changing order.

Let's trace some of these surface waves and see what effects they may be causing:

• *Population dynamics.* Demographic shifts, such as the increase in the proportion of older people, change the demand for medical services, change the tax base, and change buying patterns for a range of options such as leisure and vacations, housing, and travel. Increases at middle age ranges can cause "career pile-up" problems as an oversupply of experienced people compete for higher jobs. A decline in the number of adolescents and teenagers reduces demand for discretionary purchases such as rock music, movies, toys, and video games. Increasing economic stress and social deterioration in inner cities increase crime rates, with enormous direct and secondary impacts. Virtually all businesses are affected in some way by demographic shifts, and every strategy process should look closely at them.

• *Fracturing of mass markets.* As demographic and psychographic differences become apparent among customers for many products and services, suppliers offer more and more differentiated versions; this has the effect of causing so-called mass markets to disintegrate into separate submarkets. Witness the example of magazine publishing: In the 1960s there were relatively few mass-circulation magazines. As advertisers discovered they could target their messages better with television, the decline in ad revenues led to the decline of mass print media and the rise of many very specialized magazines. Magazines for female bowlers, teenage skateboarders, runners, golfers, photographers, and wood-carvers have replaced mass-circulation magazines. Food products, clothing, music—almost all the so-called mass markets you can think of—are breaking down into their constituent submarkets. Customer access becomes much more a matter of careful targeting.

• *Pluralism as the new customer reality.* Any one product or service draws different responses from different kinds of customers; there is no one "customer" any longer. These differences in response have always been there; it is only recently that firms are realizing the implications of the differences, and learning to tailor their offerings more directly. Hotels find that frequent business travelers have different priorities than honeymooners, who have different wants than families with children, who have different wants than retired couples, and so on. Firms are now talking about "micromarketing" and "mass-customizing," that is, customizing the offering to the individual; the ultimate market segment is becoming one individual customer.

• *Increasing complexity of customer entities.* The standard, statistical customer described in the marketing textbook is less and less common; many businesses now realize that their customers also have customers. For example, the hospital can no longer consider the doctor the only customer; the patient is the customer's customer. The third-party paying organization also wants to be treated as a customer. Insurance companies sell policies through agents and brokers; who is the customer, the agent or the person who buys the policy? The answer: both. Airlines sell their tickets both directly to the flier and also through travel agencies; they must win and keep the business of both.

• *Breaking up of traditional megacorporations.* As mass markets disintegrate and product differentiation breaks up the playing field, the large single-product firms lose their traditional advantages of concentration of capital and economies of scale. It sometimes becomes a case of "dis-economies" of scale. Huge firms like IBM, General Motors, Kodak, and Procter & Gamble have trouble sustaining their market power. More and more, megasize will become a handicap as shock waves and surface waves restructure business realities.

• *Migration of labor-intensive industries.* As labor intensive, low-value-added industries tend to migrate outward from the developed countries to third-world countries with low labor costs, the traditional industrial bases of the former manufacturing economies begin to disintegrate and lose their economic clout. When sugar growers find their production costs 150 percent more than the world price for their product, they can no longer produce it in first-world labor environments. The same is true of other labor-intensive food processing operations such as pineapples, coconuts, and other exotic foods. Complex, interwoven partnerships that ignore national boundaries cause manufacturing operations to shift according to cost structures and political influences. This leaves the more knowledge-intensive and skill-intensive processes in the advanced economies, and the dislocation of low-skilled manual workers there creates many social side effects.

• *Acceleration of digital information technology.* With high-speed, low-cost communication made possible by digital technology, and the developing marriage of computers and communications in a digital world, we have the rise of "virtual organizations," which exist only by virtue of the communication pathways that link the participants to a common purpose. There are virtual organizations inside most large firms, and virtual organizations that operate globally, such as international stockbrokerages, currency traders, and import-export firms. The major securities markets of the world are linked through the effects of instantaneous news reporting and world-wide quotation and order-placing systems. Corporations are taking advantage of global communications to give themselves worldwide presence. The island nation of Singapore has rec-ognized the potential impact of fiber-optic communication technology and has decided to transform itself into an "intelli-gent island," with coast-to-coast communication pathways, digital information utilities, and a huge data utility that will give businesses a competitive edge in world markets.

• *Globalization of business dealings.* A person in Stockholm who instructs a bank to transfer funds to another person's bank in Helsinki may not realize that the transaction goes into outer space, with electronic signals bounced off satellites, transferred through a computer network in Brussels, and end-ing up at its destination. The shoes bought by a person in Montreal may have gone from a leather producer in Texas to a tanning operation in Argentina, to an assembly factory in Italy, to an exporter in Spain, to an importer in New York, to a wholesale distributor in Ontario, and finally to a retail store in his or her neighborhood. Commerce now largely ignores na-tional boundaries. American trade unionists who push for restrictions on imported Japanese cars are befuddled to learn that most of the parts on the car they are attacking are manu-factured in the United States, and it may be assembled there as well. It is no longer clear what someone means by saying a product is Japanese, American, German, or French.

Some of these surface waves may be powerful enough in certain industries to qualify as shock waves for some enter-prises; that is, they force a restructuring of the basic realities that enterprises must face. Others are at least strong enough to change the dynamics of markets and can shift the fortunes of one competitor relative to another.

New Structural Options

Now we need to ask another, very crucial question: What basic structural changes in business dynamics are taking shape, caused by the environmental changes just enumerated? What is happening on the macro scale that is driving so many organizations toward a new model of doing business, and what is the essence of that new model?

Here we enter into the realm of conceptual speculation, and I acknowledge that the answer offered here to the questions just presented is my own particular worldview. I am content to leave it to those who read this to make up their own minds whether it offers a valid basis for understanding the new business realities.

The germ of an explanation, and the elements of a new model, come at least partly from the view developed by Peter F. Drucker in his landmark book *Post-Capitalist Society*. Drucker skillfully traces the long sweep of commercial history through three stages: (1) the "pre-capitalist" old days of the craft-based industries in which *secret knowledge* and skill were the primary asset, (2) the "capitalist" period in which *encoded knowledge* and skill (i.e., technology) could be transferred and used to organize very large and complex capital-based business operations, and (3) the now-emerging "post-capitalist" period in which the *deployment of knowledge* itself supersedes the control of capital in importance.

In the post-capitalist period, Drucker believes, it makes little difference who owns the factories, the real estate, the heavy machinery, or the facilities. Whereas the capitalist objective was maximizing the economic return on owned capital, the post-capitalist objective is maximizing *return on knowledge*.

Whereas the contribution of management was formerly to organize and direct the deployment of labor and capital, in the post-capitalist era it is becoming the creation of value through the deployment of knowledge. Whereas power and influence in organizations formerly derived from the amount of capital and labor under one's control, that is, the size of one's department, power and influence now stem increasingly from the leverage of value-creating knowledge.[1]

There is an intriguing motif threading through many of the newly emerging business practices, and it seems to validate this notion of knowledge-based organizations and the notion of technology as displacing capital in fundamental importance. Let's look at some of the new structural options being presented by the surface waves previously described:

• *Outsourcing.* Organizations are separating whole parts of their operations and having them done by outside providers; this goes beyond simply purchasing traditional services. Demographers have identified a growing "contingent workforce," composed of people who work part-time through agencies or who work as outside contractors for particular services. "Telecomputing" firms, for example, persuade large customers to virtually close down their internal data processing departments, get rid of their computers, and do all of their computer work over dedicated phone lines to a computer center many miles away. Many businesses emerging from the cost-cutting agony of a recession find it more economical to hire out various services rather than restaff their organizations.

• *The move from ownership to partnership.* There is no longer a compulsion to own all resources under one roof, as with the traditional corporate structure. Outsourcing is one component of this trend, but there are others. These days it is much more common for firms seeking to get into new ventures to seek out alliances, coventures, and partnerships with other firms already established in the game. Often this is a way to get going more quickly, reduce the costs of the learning process, and avoid the risks of irreversible resource commitments. The company organization chart, if drawn to show the complete operation, looks more like a flatter, network-type chart now than a hierarchical command structure. The formal boundaries of the company are not necessarily distinct any longer.

• *The change from capital manipulation to knowledge manipulation.* Owning large chunks of "frozen" capital, such as factories, manufacturing facilities, retail outlets, corner banks, ships, trains, and trucks is becoming more and more a liability than an advantage as the shock waves change the rules of the game. The customer mailing list is a higher-cost and higher-value asset than the computer hardware that stores and manipulates it. Leasing capital items from others, buying into part of someone else's capacity, and paying royalties or commissions to others who create part of the value can keep the organization more agile, able to shift the deployment of its resources much more rapidly when the primary resource is knowledge and not massive chunks of depreciating plant and equipment.

- *The displacement of "thing" organizations by knowledge organizations.* The three changes just enumerated—outsourcing, partnership versus ownership, and knowledge manipulation versus capital manipulation—mean that the focus of attention in defining the organization is no longer strictly capital and output; the focus is less on what the enterprise has and produces, and more on how it adds value. The emerging success motif is to leverage the capital resources owned by various other firms by "wrapping" it with a conceptual "envelope" that adds value synergistically through knowledge. As technology becomes more sophisticated and the kinds of value that businesses can deliver becomes more imaginative and diversified, an increasing proportion of the people in the organization are dealing with knowledge instead of things. Manufacturing firms have always had to have "knowledge departments" such as finance, purchasing, and personnel, but now the "knowledge overhead" required in most organizations is growing as the nature of the value they create changes. And, of course, there are many organizations that are almost totally information-intensive, such as banks, insurance companies, brokerages, data processing units, consulting firms, research organizations, educational institutions, and government agencies. Clearly, thing organizations and thing workers are now in the minority.

- *The displacement of resource power by knowledge power.* With more-complex organizations, the simple equation of political power with resources under control is breaking down. It is no longer axiomatic that the executive who has the largest bloc of employees under his or her command, or the most expensive plant and equipment, will make the most money and have the most clout. Other factors now enter into the power formula, in particular the leverage one exerts over the value-creating processes, which may involve very few people and little or no hard capital.

- *The shift of organizations from static forms to chaotic forms.* Scientists refer to "chaos theory," which is a mathematical method for describing how systems such as organizations evolve and change. A static organization is one that changes very little and whose operating state of affairs is very predictable at a given time on a given day. For example, if we were to be shown around a soft-drink bottling plant by the plant manager on a certain day, and then visit again a month or so later, or even a year later, we could probably predict fairly accurately what we would see on the subsequent visit. It is likely that not very much would change. A chaotic organization, on the other hand, is one whose structure and processes are in a state of flux, or metamorphosis. What it looks like on one particular day is not a very good basis for predicting what it will look like twelve months later, or perhaps even a few months later. The static organization makes its best contribution through minimizing change, variation, and ambiguity. The chaotic organization may have to *maximize* change, variation, and ambiguity to accomplish its ends. Neither is necessarily better; they are just different kinds of solutions.

• *The change in work from compliance to contribution.* Fewer and fewer workers now fall into the category of task doers, that is, those who perform tasks that are fully predesigned and require little or no added value in the form of knowledge, judgment, creativity, or strategy. There are still jobs like that around, but they are progressively being replaced with technology solutions such as computers, robots, and automatic teller machines.

With the ever increasing sophistication of the value-creating processes used in business, "labor" is no longer an adequate label. The operative word is becoming *people*. The concept of *discretionary effort* is emerging as a key element of value creation, in which the employee must be free to use his or her own commonsense skills and ideas to solve problems and exceed customer expectations. The difference between labor and people is in the differences between people themselves— their skills, experience, ideas, know-how, work styles, career ambitions, and motivators. Just as we have to learn to see an individual in every customer, we have to learn to see an individual in every working person. One of the main jobs of leadership is to help people understand the contributions they can make, help them realize what they're really good at as individuals, and help them grow toward the contributions they are capable of making.

• *Increasing the emphasis on stewardship and responsibility.* Jan Carlzon, chief executive of Scandinavian Airlines System, claims that capitalizing on people energy depends on creating a contract for personal responsibility. And that responsibility, he believes, starts with knowledge and information. "A person without information," Carlzon asserts, "cannot act responsibly. A person with information cannot help acting responsibly." The age-old problem of "how to motivate the employees" will never be solved as long as executives think of motivation as something they are supposed to do to people. Once they understand that motivated behavior is a response to perceived meaning and value, and that people will take charge of results when they believe in what they are doing, they leave behind archaic concepts like motivation. They move toward more-powerful concepts like the creation and management of meaning.

Three Business Models: Pre-Capitalist, Capitalist, and Post-Capitalist

Each of the three economic eras mentioned by Drucker, that is, the pre-capitalist, capitalist, and post-capitalist, brought its own thinking processes about how business should be structured. It is this evolution in the structuring of resources and relationships that is causing havoc with many businesses, and causing confusion in the minds of many business leaders.

The picture gets quite a bit clearer when you put the three structural models side by side: the pre-capitalist model, the capitalist model, and the post-capitalist model, as shown in Figure 3-1. Let's look at each one briefly, and then compare them.

1. *The pre-capitalist, or cottage industry, model,* which arose during the Middle Ages and prevailed for hundreds of years. Once agriculture had become sufficiently productive that many people were freed from working the land, they began to make and sell useful things to one another. As shown in Figure 3-1a, the triangular combination of the craftsman (a skilled person), the cottage (the primitive home-factory), and the craft

Figure 3-1. Three business models.

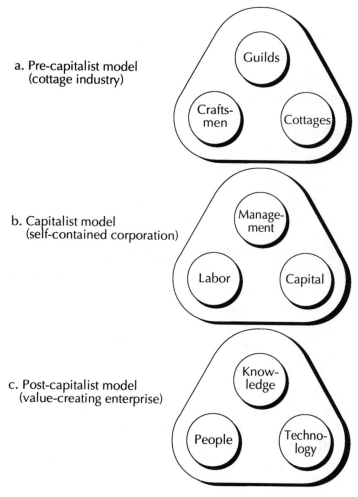

a. Pre-capitalist model
   (cottage industry)

b. Capitalist model
   (self-contained corporation)

c. Post-capitalist model
   (value-creating enterprise)

guild formed a miniature political-economic model. People at first sold their products willy-nilly in unsophisticated local marketplaces, but with the rise of the craft guilds they became more sophisticated marketers, able to do business on a larger scale. The cottage model is still alive and well today in a number of industries. Even the guilds have survived, in many cases evolving into trade associations.

2. *The capitalist, or corporation, model,* doing business on a

huge scale by concentrating vast amounts of capital and labor in one place, that is, the factory. A number of developments had to appear to make this possible: the concept of standardized products with identical, interchangeable parts; mass-production methods; large-scale energy transformation systems like the steam engine; teachable skills and methods that circumvented the secrecy and parochial turfism of the trade guilds; the concept of management as the job of organizing and directing labor and capital on a large scale; and the advent of merchant banks and fractional-reserve banking that permitted the deployment of money as a form of capital. All of this led to the corporation as a *self-contained organization,* with all of the functions of product design, development, manufacturing, marketing, and support under one entity. As shown in Figure 3-1b, the triangular combination of labor, capital, and management forms the essence of the capitalist model.

   3. *The post-capitalist model, or the value-creating enterprise,* with a much more diversified network of resources, often with less distinct boundaries than self-contained corporate structures. Ownership of capital gives way to partnerships that leverage resources, regardless of who has custody of them. As Figure 3-1c shows, the triangular combination of people, technology, and knowledge transcends the conventional labor-capital-management model. Conventional management gives way to knowledge-based leadership, conventional capital gives way to technology and the treatment of capital as simply one part of the value-creation arrangement, and conventional labor gives way to "people" in the sense that a great deal of work now requires more than manual process, engaging as it does various interpersonal skills, knowledge and initiative, situational judgments, and "emotional labor" such as dealing with customers who may be distressed, angry, ill, or mentally disturbed.

   If all of this so far seems a bit too theoretical for you, please hang on: We're almost there. We're coming to the key questions: (1) How does the post-capitalist model apply to your business? (2) What part can it play in formulating your strategic success model? and (3) What structuring options might it provide to help you surf the shock waves, exploit the trends, and manage the events in the business environment your enterprise will face in the future? We need to understand the post-capitalist model just a bit better in order to answer those questions.

Referring again to Figure 3-1, let's simplify the comparison of the three models. First, bear in mind that the post-capitalist model is not pushing the other two off the stage. It is merely joining them in the limelight. It is an additional option for structuring resources. Likewise, the capitalist model joined the cottage model on the stage rather than getting rid of it. For example, parts of the huge travel industry work on the pre-capitalist cottage model. Thousands of mom-and-pop travel agencies around the world, typically staffed by fewer than ten people, sell billions of dollars worth of airline tickets, cruise vacations, hotel bookings, and car rentals. Certainly there are large corporate agencies, but even those operate at least partially as cottage producers.

The same applies to most of the insurance business. Although a few large carriers supply the underwriting resources for the policies, thousands of small agencies sell the "product" and service the customers. Much of the tax and accounting business works the same way. Despite the existence of vast megaretailers, much of the retail industry also works on the cottage model.

Indeed, the 11,000 McDonald's restaurants operate more like cottage businesses than like one giant corporation. They are absolutely local in their customer communities, and many of them are privately owned as franchises.

At the same time, however, McDonald's is also probably an ideal example of the post-capitalist model of the value-creating enterprise. The difference between 11,000 unrelated hamburger stores and the total McDonald's franchise is in two essential ingredients: (1) worldwide brand recognition, and (2) the integrated supply of raw materials and services to the stores with tremendous economies of scale. The reason a business owner pays two or three times as much for a McDonald's franchise as he or she might pay for a similar, unbranded hamburger store is that on opening day there is a virtual guarantee of a full stream of customers who have no doubt about the value they can expect to receive. Most studies show that franchise businesses have a first-year survival rate at least three to five times higher than those that start from scratch.

Think about the example of McDonald's for a moment and you'll see that the post-capitalist model that it represents can actually incorporate both the pre-capitalist and capitalist models all in one. The individual stores are the cottages, the supporting logistical and marketing structure is the corporate component, and the franchise concept extends the model to the level of a value-creating enterprise. The value-creating enterprise can make use of networks or relationships of cottage producers, large corporate structures, and an intangible third element: *the enhancement of value through knowledge.*

At this point, an element of confusion might set in. One could ask: Don't most industries fit the definition of value-creating enterprises with their relationships of suppliers, distributors, sellers, and value-adding middlemen? Aren't they all working together to enhance value? The answer is: in most cases, no, although they could be.

Returning to the example of the travel industry, we can see that it is mostly just an assortment of individual businesses that buy and sell from, to, and through one another. Some are huge corporations such as airlines, cruise lines, and hotel operators, and others are small cottage players like local tour operators and travel agencies. But nothing like the McDonald's franchise concept exists to connect them together synergistically. In almost every industry, trade associations try to create synergy by promoting cooperation and pushing political interests, but they are still acting more like the pre-capitalist guilds than enhancing value through knowledge. Most industries have enormous opportunities for enterprise thinking that goes beyond their traditional structures and relationships for commerce.

From Organization to Enterprise

Do you begin to see the implications of the post-capitalist, value-creating enterprise for the new business environment? It goes beyond the individual structuring options such as outsourcing, partnering, strategic alliances, and organizational reengineering. Those are really just options for arranging the processes. The really important concept is the shift from self-contained organization to value-creating enterprise. The traditional organization chart gets replaced by something like an enterprise map, as in Figure 3-2.

More and more leaders, especially those who operate internationally, are learning to think in enterprise terms. In the process of "reinventing government," some public-sector leaders are adopting enterprise models for the total community they serve. For example, the government of Singapore holds a major interest in a development company that has plans to virtually clone the design of the city as an economic enterprise in Suzhou, China, near Shanghai. Using the "software" of the Singapore concept, that is, the social and commercial models, political partnership between government and business, and city-state management practices, the developers hope to create a successful first-world enterprise with the best of Singapore's unparalleled growth and managed economy.

Another interesting example of a company that has redefined its business concept and its operating relationships in terms of a value-creating enterprise is the Swedish furniture firm IKEA. Starting with the elegantly simple idea of selling assemble-it-yourself furniture made in attractive Scandinavian designs at substantially lower prices than conventional furni-

Figure 3-2.   From organization to enterprise.

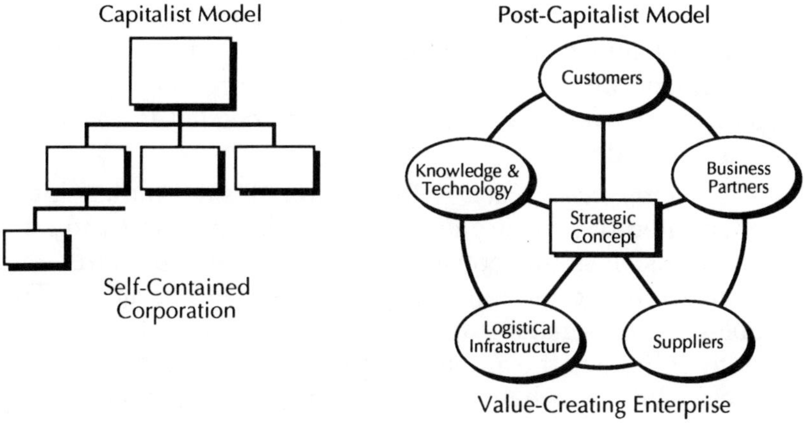

Capitalist Model

Self-Contained Corporation

Post-Capitalist Model

Customers

Knowledge & Technology

Business Partners

Strategic Concept

Logistical Infrastructure

Suppliers

Value-Creating Enterprise

© 1993 Karl Albrecht/The TQS Group.

ture, IKEA has expanded beyond its home market to a worldwide network of over one hundred stores. With revenues of over $4 billion and recession-defying rates of growth in sales and profitability, the company has reinvented the whole constellation of roles that exist between the customer, IKEA as the retail supplier, and a network of over 1,800 item suppliers around the world.

IKEA's concept is an excellent example of the deployment of knowledge in an enterprise model. It has used the simple driving objective of creating quality furniture at low prices to develop a unique network of designers, suppliers, warehouses, and retail stores all keyed to the same principle. The firm's success model revolves around several critical points of focus:

1. *Design*. IKEA utilizes clever, careful, well-executed designs that can be manufactured at low costs, while still providing high value in style, finish, and durability. IKEA designers work relentlessly to find ways to reduce the costs of fabrication, assembly, shipping, warehousing, and retailing. They work with a wide range of suppliers, many in Eastern Europe, helping each one develop the necessary orientation to cost-conscious, high-quality design.

2. *Distribution*. While many experts advise that a company reduce its suppliers to the smallest number possible, IKEA succeeds by having the right product made by just the right supplier. Indeed, IKEA designers may select several firms to produce the individual parts of a single item of furniture. They bring all finished products together into an ultrasophisticated network of fourteen warehouses. Using the latest techniques of inventory control and distribution planning, they make sure products are available when and where needed to meet customer demand.

3. *Information technology*. By linking all sales outlets into a sophisticated communication system, IKEA planners can track sales almost instantaneously, analyze demand patterns, and optimize the use of transport and warehouse facilities. This enables them to match supply more closely with demand and thereby minimize the amount of inventory in the pipeline. All of these techniques help to hold down operating costs, thereby strengthening the price advantage over conventional furniture.

4. *Customer participation.* The IKEA business concept views the customer as a key player in the overall creation of value. Going beyond the prosaic definition of knock-down furniture, the company carefully educates its customers in the ways of getting maximum value. At the retail stores, everything humanly possible is done to make it easy for the customers to play their part. This includes a pleasant shopping environment with coffee shops and child-care facilities, realistic display of furniture in natural "in-use" settings, easy-to-use order forms and notepads for sketching and planning, easy pickup and carry-out of products in cartons, and even the loan of car-top carriers so customers can easily get their products home.

Note that virtually all of these critical dimensions of the IKEA business model revolve around two basic precepts: *value* and *knowledge.* By distributing the necessary information and knowledge throughout the enterprise network, all the way out to the customer, the company has put together a value-creation concept that capitalizes on that knowledge. Instead of the standard self-contained corporation model of business, IKEA has developed a value-creating enterprise model, making best use of the cottage-industry model (suppliers), the corporate model (design, warehousing, distribution, and retailing), and the enterprise model (information and knowledge that links together the whole system).

According to Goran Carstedt, head of IKEA's North American operation and formerly head of Volvo Sales in Sweden:

> The problem of creating superior value these days calls for original thinking. You can't just drift along and hope for the best. The game is changing, and you must learn the new rules of the game. At IKEA, we want to think of ourselves as in a perpetual learning process, sort of a "virtuous circle" of experience, learning from that experience, and then evolving our value premise to ever higher levels.

Swedish Management consultant Richard Normann, director of the SMG Group in Paris, comments on the IKEA business concept:

The work-sharing, co-productive arrangements the company offers to customers and suppliers alike force both to think about value in a new way—one in which customers are also suppliers (of time, labor, information, and transportation), suppliers are also customers (of IKEA's business and technical services), and IKEA itself is not so much a retailer as the central star in a constellation of services, goods, design, management, support, and even entertainment.

The result: IKEA has succeeded, arguably, in creating more value per person (customer, supplier, and employee) and in securing greater total profit from and for its financial and human resources than all but a handful of other companies in any consumer industry.[2]

This enterprise concept is a new and unfamiliar way of thinking for many traditionally raised business leaders. Long accustomed to thinking in terms of corporate models with fixed boundaries, many of them are just beginning to sense the implications of this new way of deploying knowledge and resources.

For the remainder of the discussion in this book, the word *enterprise*, used to describe business operations, will serve to emphasize the value-creating synergy of the post-capitalist model. In focusing on your own enterprise, and on the northbound train concept that will make it a success, it is up to you to think through the possibilities and choose a strategic concept for deploying resources that is right for the business environment you intend to exploit.

Notes

1. Peter F. Drucker, *Post-Capitalist Society* (New York: HarperBusiness, 1993).
2. Richard Normann and Rafael Ramirez, "From Value Chain to Value Constellation: Designing Interactive Strategy," *Harvard Business Review*, July–August 1993.

Chapter 4

The Design of Meaning: Piecing Together the Strategy Puzzle

Fanatic: a person who redoubles his effort when he has lost sight of his aim.

Anonymous

Myths and Misconceptions About Setting Direction

In the Western business world most conventional thinking about "strategic planning," that is, setting goals and making plans to achieve them, is misguided and obsolete. Many organizations waste enormous amounts of time and precious intellectual energy trying to plan and forecast their futures. They create grandiose strategic plans, supported by elaborately detailed budgets, resource estimates, tactical plans, and timetables, most of which ultimately have little connection to the success of the business.

The history of the academic discipline known as technological forecasting tells us that it is pointless to write plans for an uncertain future. Technological forecasting is more famous for what it has failed to predict than for what it has predicted. Most of the major technological phenomena that shape our lives, such as jet aircraft, television, the computer microchip, nuclear weapons, and satellite communications, were largely unforeseen until the means for achieving them became apparent. While it is an interesting and stimulating intellectual process, forecasting is more valuable for generating possibilities and forming scenarios than for making plans.

To make matters worse, many organizations have planning systems that are bottom-heavy. They spend a great deal of time and effort getting all of the divisional and departmental tactical plans written up, but little or no time thinking about the basic strategy or direction of the business. In one American gas and electric utility company, the planning process used an elaborate system of unit plans, staffing levels, project timetables, and expenditure schedules. The chief executive personally reviewed all plans and budgets down to the departmental level. He also personally allocated expenditure levels, so the planners always ended up using the numbers he gave them in place of their own.

Nobody knew why it was necessary to go through all of the planning, since the boss was the ultimate planner. Labor costs made up the bulk of most of their budgets, and most of them already had a predetermined number of slots, so there seemed little point in going through all the planning rigmarole. But they'd been doing it for so many years that they kept at it by sheer inertia.

The irony of the situation was that the company had a very detailed tactical planning process but virtually no *strategy formulation* process. The executives had not assembled themselves in any kind of retreat or strategy conference in nearly ten years. I was asked to help them develop a strategy formulation approach and to begin the process of dealing with the most pressing strategic issues. As the executives refocused their attention on the shock wave issues and the trends and events in the business environment, they found it easier to loosen up the tactical planning process and delegate more of the leadership for operational results to the tactical managers.

There are other consequences of the planning mind-set that can impair the organization's ability to ride the shock waves, exploit trends, and manage events in the environment. For example, many budgeting systems, perhaps most, make it very difficult to redeploy resources toward new opportunities or changed priorities. It seems that once the budget has been approved and each unit leader knows what resources he or she has to work with, there is a tendency to interpret attempts to redeploy resources as a sign of poor planning. The rationale seems to be that if you were really a good planner you would have allowed for this project or investment when you prepared your budget. Never mind that this fabulous opportunity has just emerged, or that you've just discovered something that opens a door to winning more of the customer's business, or you've just come up with a great idea for solving a long-standing problem in your business. You're not a good planner.

Many organizational leaders tend to mistake budgeting for planning. In government agencies, for example, where budgets are mostly made up of labor costs, the typical unit leader simply extrapolates current-year costs to the next year, with corrections for salary adjustments and cost-of-living factors. They all dutifully put together their budgets, with a few minor changes, and the process goes on from year to year. This kind of activity-based budgeting deludes people into thinking they're planning, but in fact there is often little or no planning going on.

A worse mistake, usually, is to create a planning department, on the premise that planning is such a detailed, labor-intensive process that the enterprise needs specially appointed planners to do it. Typically, planning departments tend to become little domains of their own, with their outputs either ignored or accepted without question and not really acted upon. In one large telecommunications company, the annual business planning process had become so overstaffed and bureaucratized that it took on a life of its own. In just one division we were working with, each of the thirteen general managers had a full-time planner on staff. All of the planners in this and the other business divisions belonged to a kind of intellectual cartel that did all the planning for the organization.

The corporate-level planners demanded ever more detailed plans and more and more backup data, to the point that the division planners were unable to complete their plans within one planning cycle. In other words, it was taking them thirteen months to produce a one-year plan. The process cycle started

with the corporate group publishing a set of planning guidelines, typically a thick loose-leaf binder with about one hundred pages of material. The guidelines for producing the plan
took more paper than any reasonable strategic plan itself ought
to occupy. And the detailed operational plans were even worse.

During the executive strategy retreat, in which the leaders
were reexamining the entire destiny of the division, the subject
of the planning process had to be faced. When every one of
the general managers finally admitted that he had not actually
read his own plan, it became obvious that the planning process
had become completely detached from reality. In fact, several
of the planners lamented that they had become more or less a
"shadow government" to the executive leadership hierarchy, a
role they definitely did not feel comfortable with.

The executives eventually decided to virtually dismantle
the nightmarish process and to substitute a vastly simplified
process based on a very simple strategy statement, a few key
result areas, and a set of simple business targets. This rethinking of the process for setting direction opened up the way for a
much more creative redefinition of the group's whole approach
to its business.

From Planning to Futuring

There is a better way to think about the future. We need to
change the vocabulary we use to think and talk about guiding
our businesses into the future. *Planning* is the appropriate word
for designing a set of actions to achieve a clearly defined
outcome, when you have high certainty about the situation in
which the actions will take place and nearly full control of the
factors that ensure success in achieving the outcome. You need
a plan if you're going to build a bridge, fly an airplane,
transplant a kidney, open a new office in a foreign city, or
launch a new product.

But if you're going to venture into a marketplace in a
formerly communist country, move from a national presence
to a global marketplace, or defend your core business in the
face of massive technological and competitive changes, you
need something beyond planning. You need a thinking process

that is exploitive rather than deterministic. For want of a better word, let's simply call it *futuring*.

Planning, as it is conventionally done, has little to offer in any highly ambiguous venture. The elaborate documents, forecasts, action plans, and timetables are often nothing more than an intellectual mirage. In some cases, the illusion of precision they create can distract you from concentrating on the means for achieving your success. They can misfocus your attention on following the plans rather than on exploiting opportunities, most of which will certainly not be in the plans.

If you've ever had the assignment of trying to prepare a plan for launching a new business, or for undertaking a completely unfamiliar or unprecedented commercial venture, you've probably experienced the uncomfortable sense of ambiguity about setting revenue targets and other outcomes. How can a start-up business project a first-year revenue goal when nobody has ever done what the business intends to do? Who has the experience and knowledge to call upon? What's the point of putting some numbers on paper and torturing them until they add up to a first-year profit, or whatever success criterion one feels impelled to meet? It's an exercise in self-delusion.

Dyed-in-the-wool corporate planners will at this point respond reflexively to this question with, "Yes, but you have to have *something* to go on. You can't just decide to launch the venture without defining the criteria for success." That is certainly true, and that point is the basis for the difference between planning and futuring. The professional planner demands, "What's the alternative to preparing a plan?" The futurist replies, "Defining a rationale for success."

Think of futuring as an approach that explicitly acknowledges the fact that you cannot know the future with certainty. You probably cannot even anticipate the most important changes that lie in store for you. You will face shock waves, trends, and events you cannot control and in most cases cannot predict. Futuring should acknowledge the fact that hitting the exact targets of any plan you could write would be a sheer accident. So it sets aside the planning process and substitutes for it a more versatile, adaptive, proactive, and responsive *action-strategy* process. Futuring is not as easy as writing a plan and putting it into the filing cabinet. It is a constantly active mental process that generates action strategies for capitalizing on the unfolding environment.

With a futuring approach, we need outcome measures, or *critical indicators*, that help us gauge the effectiveness of our action strategies. But we do not delude ourselves into thinking we have set realistic goals and are working to achieve them. Instead, we are developing action strategies to exploit what is happening in the environment, and we are using the critical indicators as criteria for further deciding what to do. We don't victimize ourselves with worries about succeeding or failing. Instead, we are continually adapting to the consequences of our action strategies. It may seem like a subtle distinction, but it can be profound in its effect on our thinking processes.

From this point of view, the typical annual planning cycle that so many organizations religiously follow may actually impair their agility in responding to changes, threats, and opportunities. Writing the annual plan and budget is typically such an exhausting process that thereafter nobody wants to change it, even if some major environmental event occurs in the middle of the year.

We need *both* planning and futuring to make an enterprise successful. We need individuals skilled in both disciplines. And we need leaders who are comfortable with both. Whereas futuring is the process of deciding *how to behave* based on what's happening in the immediate and near-future environment, planning is the translation of that decision into manageable actions. Let's not feel guilty because we can't plan for a confusing and ambiguous future. But let's have the skill and discipline to continuously interpret that future into strategic actions and responses, and then let's use our planning skills to accomplish the plans that make sense. We might relate the orientation of planning to that of futuring in the following way:

Planning	*Futuring*
In planning, you must:	In futuring, you must:
• Define outcomes or goals.	• Ride shock waves.
• Determine actions.	• Exploit trends.
• Commit resources.	• Manage events.
• Aim for defined targets.	• Monitor critical indicators.

Futuring and planning must merge at the point where we can devise an action strategy and translate it into a goal or target. In this sense, planning becomes the tactical result of futuring, but we do not expect planning to solve the strategic puzzle for us. It is a dynamic puzzle, pieced together day by day, month by month, year by year—not assembled in advance in some document called a plan.

The guiding premise for this creative maneuvering is, as mentioned previously, the northbound train. With a clear understanding of who we really are, what we're capable of, what business we're in, what value we create for our customers, and how we differentiate ourselves in winning and keeping our customers, we have the means to make the most of whatever the business environment presents. This is our task for the remainder of the book: to learn how to create that success premise, the northbound train.

The Strategic Success Model: Connecting the Dots

It is not enough that the chief executive of the organization has a good idea for the future of the enterprise and the determination to see it through. The northbound train must be more than one person's idea; it must be everybody's idea. It must be the manifestation of that idea in an action format. The leadership challenge is to develop the idea, express it in compelling and useful terms so everybody in the organization can relate it to his or her personal work life, and help them translate it into action. For this reason it is very important to have a conceptual framework that can express all of the critical elements of the direction in easily understood terms and show how they interconnect.

Sometimes the executives of a firm succeed in evolving a strong concept for the success of the business but fail to "package" it effectively. They may come up with a document such as a strategy statement, a vision statement, a statement of philosophy, a values statement, a set of company principles, a mission statement, or any of a number of other ways of expressing what they want the enterprise to do, be, or become. Too often, however, even the most basic document of this kind never gets far beyond the executive suite. In other cases, it may show up around the organization, but there may be very little energy behind it and no commitment on the part of the leaders to make it come alive for people. This is sometimes the most difficult part of developing the direction and often the one least likely to be done effectively, for a number of reasons. Later we will study these pitfalls in more detail, as we develop some reliable methods for communicating the northbound train idea.

There is, of course, no one correct way to articulate the direction of an enterprise. Organizations are so vastly different in their operating environments, target markets, relationships to their customers, leadership patterns, and cultures, that each needs to express its critical success concept in its own way. However, twenty years of research and experience in strategy formulation have led me to think in terms of certain constructs, or components of meaning, that can form the basis of a conceptual architecture for direction. We need a sort of generic *strategic success model* that can serve as a starting point for creating and expressing meaning.

All of the discussion hereafter will make use of this generic strategic success model as presented in Figure 4-1. Bear in mind, however, that there is no universally accepted format. It is perfectly reasonable to arrange the components differently, or to dice up the elements of meaning into more or fewer elements, so long as the arrangement you use meets the tests of clarity, validity, and focus on success.

As Figure 4-1 illustrates, the strategic success model helps to structure meaning and direction into five levels, moving from the most abstract level of a vision for the enterprise down to the level of a few critical goals as a focus for short-term action. For this discussion, we will briefly review the overall hierarchy as a model for thinking and communicating about direction. Later we will deal with each of the major components in much more depth.

Level 1: Vision

• *Vision statement*—a shared image of what we want the enterprise to be or become, typically expressed in terms of success in the eyes of its customers or others whose approval

Figure 4-1.   The strategic success model.

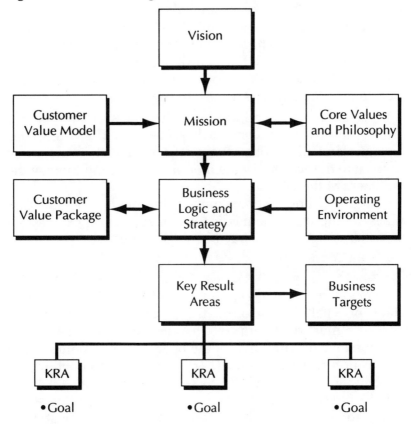

can affect its destiny. It is a determination the leaders make, which provides an aiming point for a future orientation. It answers the question, "How do we want those we care about to perceive us?" The vision statement usually implies an element of noble purpose and high values, of something considered especially worthwhile.

Level 2: Mission

• *Mission statement*—a simple, compelling statement of how the enterprise must do business. It defines who its customers are, the value premise it offers those customers, and any special means it will use to create value for them to win and keep their business.

• *Customer value model*—a set of critical factors that define customer value from the customer's point of view. Derived from careful, creative, and disciplined customer research, it tells us what value we have to provide in order to win and keep the customer's business. It may turn out to be several customer value models, one for each major variation in the constellation of customers the business aspires to serve.

• *Core values*—the critical few values to which the people in the enterprise must commit their energies. The core values are not standard "motherhood" statements; they are those essential to the accomplishment of the mission and thereby the fulfillment of the vision.

Note that both the customer value model and the core values are inputs to the mission statement, which expresses a particular design for our way of doing business.

Level 3: Strategic Concept

• *Operating environment*—a thorough and insightful explanation of what's going on in the business environment the enterprise must deal with. In Chapter 5 we will see how the "environmental scan" divides the operating environment into eight conceptual categories: (1) customer, (2) competitor, (3) economic, (4) technological, (5) social, (6) political, (7) legal, and (8) physical. All of these subenvironments offer shock waves, trends, and events which the enterprise must ride, exploit, or manage in order to succeed.

• *Business logic and strategy*—the essential logic of the business, expressed in terms of a major action premise that can maximize market share, revenue, short-run profit, long-run profit, return on investment, or whatever focus of success the leaders have chosen. In Chapter 10 we will see how the concept of business logic, expressed in the four key sublogics of (1) customer logic, (2) product logic, (3) economic logic, and (4) structural logic, can help to align the energies of the people throughout the enterprise so as to create synergy among its elements.

• *Customer value package*—the infrastructure for value creation the enterprise uses in doing business with its customers. It consists of at least the seven generic dimensions or components identified as (1) environmental, (2) sensory, (3) interpersonal, (4) procedural, (5) deliverable, (6) informational, and (7) financial. The actual form of these components varies widely from one type of business to another, but in every case the design of the CVP should be compatible with all other components of the strategic success model. Chapter 11 explains the design of this CVP in more detail.

Level 4: Strategic Initiatives

• *Business targets*—the objective indicators of business success. They may include revenue-growth targets, market-share targets, and cost-reduction targets. They may also include qualitative accomplishments like landing certain contracts, completing certain projects, gaining certain marketing rights, and so on.

• *Key result areas*—a few critical categories for action that can focus the attention of leaders and working people at all levels. These KRAs may deal with externally focused actions such as marketing, brand identity, strategic partnerships, and the like, or they may be inwardly focused action categories such as product development, cost control, resource efficiency, applying information technology, or developing the workforce. If properly chosen, these few critical KRAs will contribute to better carrying out the business strategy, executing the mission, and achieving the business targets.

Level 5: Outcomes

• *Adaptive goals*—the few critical implementing goals under each of the key result areas that define the basis for action. Adaptive goals should not be confused with business targets. I refer to them as adaptive goals because they play a part in redirecting the energy and attention of the enterprise toward the new things that must be done. Many organizations have routine business targets such as revenue levels and other key performance parameters. While those are important, they do not serve to concentrate attention on new problems and challenges. This is what the adaptive goals do, under the various key result areas.

Please take a moment to review the relationships of these components in the strategic success model. See how they flow together to establish an architecture of meaning for the enterprise. In a way, the strategy formulation process amounts to finding the answers that go into the various boxes. Unfortunately, however, too many executives and leadership teams think of it as merely filling in the squares, rather than working out the creative logic of success. The harder the organization's leaders are willing to work, the more deeply they are willing to think; and the more fundamentally they are willing to analyze every premise of the business, the more powerful the solution they are likely to create and the more meaningful will be the premise for the northbound train.

The Strategy Formulation Process: Building the Model

It is very helpful to have in mind a general flow of events, or a conceptual process for the things that have to be done in putting the strategic model together. Whether the enterprise is solidly on a successful strategic track or in need of a fundamental redefinition of itself, it is equally important to have a disciplined way to review the important shock waves, trends, and events presenting themselves. The conceptual strategy must always be on probation, and any annual strategy process must systematically reconsider all basic premises. Even if the indicated action is to maintain the present course and speed, there is danger in not carefully revisiting the strategic concept on a regular basis.

While no two strategy experts are likely to agree completely on the process flow, there are a few widely accepted components that surely belong in any strategy approach, however specific it is to a particular enterprise. The process presented here derives from a wide variety of accepted models and seems to account for just about all the major schools of thinking in business strategy. For the remainder of the discussion, we will use the model shown in Figure 4-2 as a guide.

At this point, we shall take a quick snapshot of the strategy formulation process. The following chapters will deal with each of the major components of the process in turn.

Figure 4-2. The strategy formulation process.

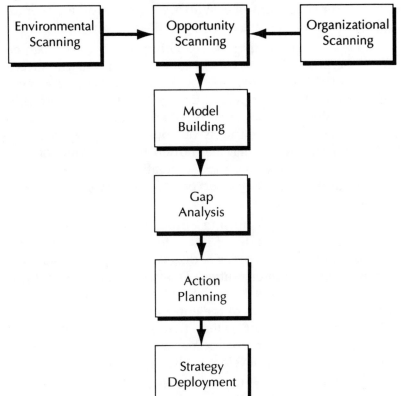

The Strategy Formulation Process

• *Environmental scanning*—a comprehensive and thoughtful study of the environment in which the enterprise must operate. It answers the question of what's happening in the business environment. It identifies the shock waves we must ride, the major trends we can exploit, and the key events we must manage.

• *Organizational scanning*—an equally comprehensive and thoughtful examination of the current state of the enterprise: its resources, its current position in its environment, its capacities and incapacities, its culture, the state of mind of its people, its leadership, and all the other characteristics that define its capacity for succeeding in its environment. This scan realistically answers questions like: Who are we? How do we operate? and What are we capable of doing outstandingly well?

• *Opportunity scanning*—a searching and creative examination of the possibilities to be considered in defining the success premise of the enterprise within its environment. It answers the question of what opportunities the shock waves, trends, or events in the environment are offering us. Some of these opportunities may be glaringly obvious, others may be speculative, and still others may be hidden from the view of most onlookers. This is very much a creative component of the process, and much of the success of the rest of the process depends on it.

• *Model building*—putting into simple and compelling terms a conceptual model of the enterprise we need to build, become, or evolve to in order to deal with the environment and capitalize on the opportunities. This *strategic success model*, as illustrated in Figure 4-1, is defined in terms of the vision, mission, and core values of the enterprise, as well as its means for delivering customer value, that is, the customer value model and the customer value package. This model becomes the essential basis for developing the organization.

• *Gap analysis*—identifying the disparity between what is and what ought to be. This means making a realistic assessment of what the enterprise has to improve on to approximate the performance of the strategic success model and identifying the specific elements of change that are necessary. Typical gaps might be, for example, the speed of the time-to-market for new products, the need for a much greater customer recognition factor in the market, the need for better application of information technology, or the need to improve cost structure and resource efficiency to meet the levels of the most important competitors.

• *Action planning*—defining the critical few key result areas for change that the organization can realistically work on during the near-term planning period. These KRAs should address the gaps discovered in the gap analysis. This also includes setting one or two critical adaptive goals under each KRA and making sure the tactical leaders at various levels of the organization align their plans as much as possible with the KRAs. The litmus test for effectively choosing KRAs and setting adaptive goals in each is the question, Will this line of effort help to close the gap between the current state of the enterprise and the strategic success model?

• *Strategy deployment*—communicating the direction throughout the organization, getting leaders at all levels comfortable with and committed to it, and helping working people understand it and what it means to them. This means giving people a part to play in working out how the strategy will be implemented at their levels and in their own areas of work.

These two basic models, the strategic success model and the strategy formulation process, go together to serve as a kit bag of tools for creating the northbound train concept. If an organization's leaders are not highly experienced in strategy formulation, they can follow these two models closely as a guide. Otherwise, they can develop their own approach and use the models merely as a check for completeness, validity, and power.

Chapter 5

The Environmental Scan: What's Going On Out There?

Men stumble over the truth from time to time,
but most pick themselves up and hurry off
as if nothing happened.

Winston Churchill

Environmental Intelligence: Your Crystal Ball

Executive teams vary considerably in the discipline with which they study their environments. The more sophisticated of them devote continuous attention to what's happening outside their doors. Some organizations even have what amount to "environmental intelligence" units. They have people with no other job but to read the signals and alert the leaders to their implications.

Many organizations, however, are remarkably out of touch with the wider world. Their executives may be so preoccupied with near-field problems and issues that they feel they have no time to think about the far field. These organizations tend to be the sitting ducks that take the worst punishment when the shock wave hits. A major shock wave may come through a particular industry only once in a decade, and nine years of complacency can leave most of the players dangerously vulnerable.

But environmental intelligence has more value than just in averting disasters. It is the very raw material for creating new opportunities as well. Indeed, it is the starting point for the whole strategy development process. The environmental scan, the first component of the model, gets us grounded in reality and may enable us to see what our competitors may not see. It is the figurative crystal ball of strategic thinking.

However, there is a lot going on in the environment of a typical business enterprise. Who can even define the environment comprehensively? Can anyone ever fully understand all of its dimensions and interpret all of its signals? Surely not. But by thinking of the environment in terms of its major components, we can at least make the challenge less daunting. We need a way to subdivide the business environment into more manageable categorical components so we can begin to organize our knowledge of it.

The Eight Critical Environments

Figure 5-1 shows a conceptual breakdown of the business environment into eight generic subenvironments. By studying the goings-on in each of them and connecting the lessons of all of them into a unified picture, we can build a solid basis in fact and a reasonable basis for speculation about what's going to happen to the players in the competitive arena.

Let's briefly visit the eight basic environments treated in the environmental scan:

1. *Customer environment*—the identity, wants, needs, behaviors, habits, values, and life situations of those who do business with you. This category is concerned with both demographic and psychographic truths about customers. It also recognizes that the enterprise may deal with complex customer entities such as businesses, governments, and groups of people, as well as simply with individuals.

What are demographic changes doing to your customer

Figure 5-1. The operating environment.

environment? Which demographic factors—such as gender, age, marital patterns, birthrates, education, economic situation, buying habits, religious patterns, mobility, and the like—have the biggest influence on your access to your customers? What psychographic changes are happening in your customer environment? How do social values—such as styles and trends; ecological awareness; health consciousness; attitudes toward institutions such as government, police, and corporations; family values; and gender relationships—condition the life environment of your customers? How do rising crime and violence influence their thinking? How are changes in the customers' own personal or business environments forcing them to change?

Get yourself mentally inside your customers' worlds and learn what they're experiencing and how they are reacting to the changes in their worlds. By studying closely what's happening *to* your customers, you can better understand and even anticipate what's happening *with* them. Are there new issues facing them, and can you translate these issues into the value premise of your business? By the way, be sure to study the customers you hope to do business with, not just the ones you're currently serving; you may discover important differences.

2. *Competitor environment*—the identity, motives, strengths, weaknesses, current behavior, and potential behavior of the other enterprises that compete for your customers' resources. It's not necessary, and usually not advisable, to build your strategic approach around what your competitors are doing; you just need to be clear about how they are approaching the customers you want to do business with.

How do the competitors array themselves in your particular industry? Are there just a few big players? Is your enterprise one of them? Or is it a "cats and dogs" industry, with no really dominant player? Are your competitors ganging up? Are they forming alliances or coventures? Are they searching for acquisitions that strengthen their customer access? Are they aggressively bringing new offerings to the market? Are they taking advantage of new technologies to do more for the customer or to drive down costs, or both? Are global competitors affecting you? Where are the other players weak or inadequate? What gaps exist? What blind spots might they have concerning customer value that you might be able to exploit?

Don't forget that in some cases, your customers themselves may become your competitors, if they "in-source" things they have been buying from you. In fact, your competition isn't limited to just the other enterprises offering to do exactly the same thing you do. The competition may be other entities in your business world that do things that could lead your customers to do less business with you.

3. *Economic environment*—the dynamics of markets, capital, critical resources, costs, prices, currency, state of the national economy, and the state of international trade, all of which may affect the buying patterns of the customers, the behavior of competitors, and the opportunities open to your own enterprise.

What are the few critical economic factors that most affect demand for what you provide? How recession-sensitive is your industry? How does it behave in boom times? On the down slope? During the comeback phase? Do global markets affect your business directly? Are your prices or costs sensitive to foreign exchange, interest rates, or investment yields? Do you depend heavily on critical materials or processes that fluctuate in price or availability? Is demand for your products or services hostage to, or derived from, other more primary economic activity? How will changes in tax policy affect your customers or your business?

What shock waves can you see coming, and how might they affect you? If you depend on a few large customers for most of your revenue, could losing one jeopardize your survival? Are there economic changes in other industries that can translate into advantage in your industry? For example, can you cannibalize business from others vying for the customer's resources?

The economic environment is a very complex one, and it helps to sort the various changes into primary and secondary effects, so you can keep the analysis to manageable proportions.

4. *Technological environment*—the range of technological events, trends, and solutions available or on the way that can improve the capability of your enterprise for creating value. This includes the study of the developers of new technologies and their likely behavior, the technology itself, and the trends associated with the application of the technology.

How are technological changes affecting your customers, and how do those changes lead to new threats or opportunities for your enterprise? Which technologies are coming fast, and which ones are dying? Are you riding the developing ones, or the dying ones? What are the long-wave changes, the ones certain to drive events for many years? What are the short-wave changes, open to debate about their long-term consequences? How long will it take to build the most valuable of these technologies into your operation?

Are there new products or processes that can jeopardize the very existence of your enterprise? What possible breakthrough, if achieved, could restructure your industry? What one technological capability could make the biggest difference in your ability to create value for your customers? Should you be investing your own resources in developing certain technologies for your needs?

5. *Social environment*—the cultural patterns, values, beliefs, trends, styles, preferences, heroes, villains, and conflicts that form the reference system of people's behavior. These may include the effects of national cultures, individual ethnic cultures within a country, and various social segments such as teenagers and people with various lifestyles. These parameters can strongly affect customer behavior as well as define the opportunities open for new market ventures.

What broad social issues or changes in attitudes might make certain products less desirable, or others more in demand? What problems of public life—such as law and order; civil rights; questions of medical ethics; family values and relationships; moral and religious issues; the role of the media; and the rights of various special-interest groups—are changing your part of the business environment?

What part does the issue of corporate social responsibility, that is, good citizenship, play in your business? How do people feel about your kind of industry or your organization? What must you rethink, what must you reevaluate, and what must you start doing differently to position your enterprise with the set of values you consider necessary?

6. *Political environment*—the processes of national, regional, and local governments, as well as various power groups that can affect the rules for doing business. This can include government intervention in particular industries, tax policies at all levels, government expenditures for certain causes, legislation aimed at implementing social policy, and regulation of various industries and trade practices. In some countries, it can even involve the basic stability or instability of the national government, effects of corruption, and the safety of the enterprise itself.

Differences in laws and policies from one regional government to another can mean that doing business can be easy in one part of a country and a nightmare in another. It may even be advisable to relocate all or part of a business operation to eliminate the negative effects of political hostility. The political environment can also include the influence of informally organized pressure groups, activist organizations, associations representing people or organizations committed to various goals, and media interest in certain issues.

7. *Legal environment*—the pattern of laws, lawmaking activity, and litigation that can affect the success of the enterprise. This can involve legal considerations of patents, copyrights, trademarks, and other intellectual property; antitrust considerations; trade protectionism; product liability; environmental liability; and employment law and litigation, including equal employment issues, sexual harassment, and the rights of employers to hire and fire at will. Clearly, some societies are more litigious than others: The United States, for example, has over twenty times more lawyers per 100,000 population than Japan. Some firms use litigation as part of their competitive strategy. The prospect of expensive or even catastrophic litigation requires that the leaders of the enterprise have a conscious risk-management approach suitable to the realities of their business.

8. *Physical environment*—the physical surroundings of the organization's facilities and operations, including the ecosystems and natural resources, availability of raw materials, transportation options, proximity to major population centers and sources of skilled talent, susceptibility to environmental disasters like earthquakes and hurricanes, and the effects of crime in the near environment. Changes in any of these factors can affect the success of the business. The location of the corporate headquarters may not be very significant, but the geographic location of offices and distribution centers to maximize customer access can be critical. Operating in a severely congested urban environment may make it more difficult to attract certain kinds of highly talented employees, who value other aspects of quality of life. For businesses that depend on natural resources such as oil, minerals, wood, water, or land access, trends in the management of these assets by governments or other custodians can have a major effect on strategic options.

Reading Your Crystal Ball

In using this environmental model, a note of caution is in order: It is important not to fall into the habit of thinking of these eight hypothetical environments as if they really were separate components. Indeed, they are not. In many cases, the most valuable insights come from discovering phenomena that weave through all of them or that transcend any imaginary, intellectual dividing line between one and another. The only value in dividing them up is to make the process of analysis more manageable. The real value is ultimately in putting them back together.

Most executive teams could do a much better job of reading their environmental crystal ball, and most could do a much better job of putting the information to use. It is quite common for the market-research "eggheads" in an organization to have a wealth of information at their disposal, and for none of the leaders of the enterprise to even know what they have. And seldom do executives deploy market intelligence throughout the organization, or even one or two levels down to the managers who could benefit from a better understanding of the business challenges facing the enterprise.

If your leadership team has a periodic formal strategy retreat, say at least as often as once a year, it is a good idea to present everybody at the meeting with a written report of the environmental scan. This document should be a masterpiece of careful selection, digestion, and interpretation of the critical elements of environmental intelligence. It should not overwhelm them with data or too much information for them to process. But every leader should be expected to understand the operating environment in some depth and be prepared to capitalize on that knowledge in the strategy development process as well as in leading his or her own unit to meet its mission.

Chapter 6

The Organizational Scan: Who Are We?

Oh wad some power the giftie gie us
To see oursels as others see us!
It wad frae monie a blunder free us,
An' foolish notion.

Robert Burns, "To a Louse"

Historicizing: How the Enterprise Became What It Is

> **his-tor-i-ciz-ing**—a process of examining the history of a business enterprise to establish a perspective for considering its possibilities for success in the future.

Historicizing is a real word, but you won't find the business-oriented definition I've given it in any dictionary. Thus defined, it's a valuable word and a valuable concept for the enterprise. Historicizing is a surprisingly engaging process that lends energy and insight to the consideration of opportunities open to the business. It creates a common starting point and a shared sense of history, and it helps newer members of the leadership team understand some of the quirks and patterns of the organization.

When the executives of the Commonwealth of Australia's Department of Administrative Services got together with us to develop their concept for the future of the organization, one of our first steps was to ask the questions, Where have we been? What brought us here? and Why do we face this particular environment and this particular set of issues?

The organization had gone through a number of wrenching changes over the previous three years, including a major downsizing, several changes in its charter, and considerable uncertainty due to debates at higher political levels about whether it should even exist. As Executive General Manager Colin McAlister puts it:

> There was a great deal of pain in the organization. Many people had devoted their careers to public service, and they wondered whether it was appreciated. Many were worried about their jobs and their futures. Executives weren't sure of their roles as leaders. And managers at all levels were feeling the stress of the uncertainty about the organization's future.
>
> We had never really stopped to reflect on the things our people had been through. We needed to come to terms with it emotionally, on a very personal basis, in order to move forward in our roles as leaders. We needed to understand our own history, and to come to peace with it.

As we progressed through a four-day strategy retreat, the realizations that emerged from the historical review became ever more powerful in shaping the concept of what the enterprise could be. They also helped to clarify the difficulties to be faced in taking a completely new business concept to 12,000 people who were already in a state of uncertainty and consternation. Most of the executives felt quite strongly that the historical perspective gave meaning and validity to the strategic thinking process.

Even a relatively young organization has probably had

certain turning points, challenges, hard times, rough spots, and possibly even crises in its history. When people review their history and take personal ownership of their background, traditions, and current momentum, they are in a better position to look at their future possibilities realistically.

Older organizations, and particularly very old ones, may have a rich heritage and history to draw on. But how many of them really capitalize on the knowledge of their past? A succession of chief executives, a growth pattern that brings many new faces into the organization, and changing times may conspire to separate people from a sense of their history. This can be a shame, because a sense of shared experience can be a powerful force in uniting people, even if the experiences they have been through were difficult or painful ones.

A historicizing step can be a very valuable starting point for an executive strategy retreat, particularly if the leaders have not done such a thing recently, or if there are many new players on the executive team. By reflecting on the organization's past and expressing clearly the realizations they take from it, they can have a sounder perspective for thinking about their opportunities.

What Are We Really Good At?

One of the most valuable things you can learn from the organizational scan, and especially from historicizing, is what you shouldn't be trying to do. Quite a few organizations get themselves into painful and unproductive situations by trying to enter markets they have no business being in, create products or services they don't have the expertise for, and manage operations they have no understanding of or affinity for.

In their landmark book *In Search of Excellence*, Tom Peters and Bob Waterman identified one of the eight critical success factors for businesses as the determination to "stick to the knitting."[1] Every organization seems to have a primary capacity for doing a few things well, but certainly not for doing many things well. A degree of overconfidence, overoptimism, simple naïveté, or even desperation may impel its leaders to want to diversify into new territory. Too often they underestimate the challenges involved and overestimate the organization's capacity for operating on unfamiliar ground.

And too often their own history shows clearly that they are not good at what it will take to succeed in the new venture. If only they would take a realistic look at their strengths, they would find that the list doesn't include the critical success factor that is required. This is not to say that no organization can ever learn to do something very different from its familiar pursuits. But it is easy to underestimate the challenges involved.

The most common form of this blunder is an attempt at nonsynergistic diversification, to coin a technical term. In other words, a company may acquire a business that operates in a market or in a manner of doing business that is completely disparate and unrelated to its own. There is no easy way the two kinds of businesses can share the same customer base, the same technology, the same marketing channels, the same employee skills, or the same executive know-how and philosophical direction.

For a number of years Sears Roebuck, the Chicago-based retailing giant, struggled to make sense of its ownership of the stockbrokerage firm Dean Witter. It was a classic case of an acquisition made from the point of view of the balance sheet, not from the point of view of creating market synergy or achieving greater customer access. Similarly, Sears owned Allstate Insurance Company, another enterprise completely unrelated to retailing. There was a feeble rationale that asserted that people passing through a retail store might be customers for investments or insurance, but it never went far.

Avon Products, the American personal-care and cosmetics marketer that operates largely through a vertical network of amateur door-to-door salespeople, somehow got the idea that owning a medical products company would be a good move. As their core market began to level off and sales stagnated, their executives began looking for diversification opportunities. So they made a deal with entrepreneur John Foster to buy out his company, Foster Medical. After less than a year of trying to function in the Avon corporate environment, Foster left in exasperation and went back to the entrepreneurial world. Not long afterward, Avon ran the medical business into the ground, eventually dismantling it and taking huge write-offs.

American aerospace and military suppliers have been learning the same lesson in trying to reorient themselves for peacetime operation. The idea that sword-making equipment can just as easily make plowshares doesn't seem to hold up to reality. Organizations geared to marketing huge contracted development projects to a handful of very large buyers with deep pockets, that is, military and other federal agencies, often don't have a clue how to create the marketing infrastructure to bring commercial products to retail customers. With the entire infrastructure of the organization designed to mirror the bureaucracy of government procurement and program management, very few of these firms have the cost-consciousness, quick reaction time, or competitive instincts to operate outside their familiar arenas.

It's becoming clear that even the megacorporations like ITT, MCA, and RJR Nabisco are not especially synergistic in the way they maintain ownership of a wide range of unrelated businesses. Conglomeration may make sense to the executives who bolt them together with other people's money, capitalizing on the size of the total balance sheet to build their own wealth and compensation, but they add no intrinsic value to the businesses they acquire. The specter of the long whip being lashed out from the distant headquarters to flay the back of the corporate chief executive who doesn't make his numbers is all too familiar. But when it comes to extending a helping hand, the whip wielder is not always up to the role.

In the context of the organizational scan, it is important to consider carefully this question of what the enterprise is capable of doing well. It doesn't mean we should never venture into unfamiliar waters, only that we need a realistic understanding of what it will really take to succeed, and a clear idea of whether we have—or can learn—what it takes.

How Do We Think?

Probably the next most valuable insight about the organization is an understanding of its collective intelligence, that is, the mind-sets, thinking processes, biases, and modes of reasoning and problem solving that go on there. Whether its leaders like to admit it or not, the fact is that most organizations have very definite dos and don'ts regarding what is thinkable and what is discussable.

During a meeting with a task force of middle managers of a large company several years ago, I watched in fascination as the group danced around an issue we all knew to be taboo in the organization. It concerned a way to diversify customer value by trading lower profitability in one area in exchange for better profitability overall. One of the more junior people asked, "Well, why don't we present the option to senior management, and see what they think?" The immediate response from one of the more experienced managers was, "Listen, if we bring that up, we're dead meat."

This was a chilling realization: They believed their personal well-being and even their careers would be jeopardized by merely discussing a possibility that seemed to offer value for the enterprise. Whether the idea ultimately had any merit was less important than the political acceptability of mentioning a taboo subject. Later, in meetings with the executive team, I surfaced the gist of the problem without identifying the source. The executives began to reflect on the intellectual culture they had evolved and began to wonder whether their own patterns of thinking were being slavishly imitated down through the ranks.

It is quite common for a particular pattern of thinking to take hold in an organization, and for the unconscious dynamics of the culture to reward those who exemplify it and punish those who don't. If the thinking pattern prevents the leaders and those who support them from considering important options for dealing with the shock waves, trends, and events that confront the enterprise, then this kind of "groupthink" can actually sink the firm.

Some organizations are run by engineers, scientists, or other technical experts. An organization in a high-tech industry or a highly specialized operation may be run by an intellectual cartel of people who specialize in that field. This may be perfectly appropriate, but it often happens that one's entitlement to speak and be taken seriously may depend on one's formal "tickets." In one nuclear-power firm I worked with, I could tell without asking which of the people around a conference table had Ph.D. degrees and which ones had only master's degrees or a lowly bachelor's, just by the unconscious nonverbal signals of deference and condescension. If you weren't a nuclear "high priest," you might not even be at the meeting.

In a completely different culture, an aircraft manufacturing firm, the tables were turned the other way. The head of the organization had come up through the manufacturing ranks, and the prevailing style of thought focused on the hard realities of manufacturing planes and parts of planes. Those who got ahead were usually people who had long experience in the shop, or substantial field operations experience. Out of a total population of over 5,000 employees, I knew of only six people who had Ph.D. degrees, and most of them would not make that fact known unless directly asked. In that culture, Ph.D.s were considered eggheads with little to contribute.

There are financial cultures, run by financially oriented people. It doesn't take long before the language of money, risk avoidance, and control becomes the norm. Anybody who speaks a different language signals that he or she is not a member of the ruling cartel. There are medical cultures, in which the only people entitled to contribute their ideas are those with clinical titles.

The vast majority of business organizations have male cultures, because males usually occupy the top slots. As psychologist Deborah Tannen points out in her book *You Just Don't Understand*, men and women tend to have different psycholinguistic reference systems. Men generally are raised on the language and metaphors of sport, warfare, and sexual conquest. Women tend to be more comfortable with a reference system that values interpersonal dynamics, human relationships, and a sense of common cause.[2] It is probably fair to say that a large portion of the brainpower available to most organizations goes unchallenged and unused because of these male-female differences.

It is a relatively rare enterprise that has freed itself from intellectual clannishness and can honor all ways of thinking and knowing. This requires that the tyranny of expertise and credentials be balanced with a respect for the contributions of nonexperts. It requires an appreciation of the enrichment that can come from people who supposedly have naïve ways of looking at the business.

Even more seriously, the effectiveness of the executive team depends heavily on the way in which its members integrate their own individual *thinking styles.* In a group of a dozen or so senior executives, there will be markedly different patterns for conceptualizing, processing information, making decisions, listening, and expressing ideas. Research into cognitive psychology has revealed a group of well-defined thinking patterns, or thinking styles, that people tend to rely on in arranging the furniture in their heads. Two people with similar thinking styles will tend to have a much easier time making themselves understood to each other than two people with very different styles.

This often explains why a chief executive will tend to favor one or more executives over the others. It is not uncommon for one or two people to have the ear of the chief and to enjoy the role of confidant, while others are more or less frozen out. It's not a matter of "telling him what he wants to hear" so much as having a comfort level with the same cognitive style. They simply hear and understand one another better, and they tend to develop a level of trust based on comfort.

The downside of this phenomenon is that it can easily degenerate to a form of cognitive bigotry in which the chief considers those with radically different thinking styles to be somehow inferior, less competent intellectually, and less worthy of being heard. Every chief executive needs to consider carefully the differing thinking patterns among the members of the team, and question seriously whether he or she might be undervaluing the views of certain individuals and overrelying on the views of others. When it comes to the problem of thinking through the complex swirl of forces going on in the business environment and sorting through the challenges and possibilities open to the enterprise, a distorted or heavily biased pattern of thinking can lead to serious market myopia and blurred corporate vision. This is actually a serious risk for most organizations.

It is quite common for the executives of an enterprise to

think of their technology as a competitive asset and yet not realize that the collective thinking patterns of the organization may be an even more influential factor in responding effectively to the environment.

A valuable part of any executive strategy retreat can be a careful consideration of the issue of how the executive team thinks. A quick look at their individual thinking styles, as well as a critical review of how these styles interact in team-level thinking, problem solving, and strategy formulation, can increase the overall effectiveness of the process immensely.[3]

What Do We Reward, Punish, and Condone?

When the pop-psychology theory of *transactional analysis* came along some years ago, a popular expression used by people applying it in organizations was "What you stroke is what you get." It means that executives, whether or not they realize it, are always influencing the behavior of people in the organization by what they do and the ways they react. Just as the culture rewards certain thinking processes and discourages others, in the ways previously described, so too does it select out certain behaviors and encourage or condone others.

The term *condone* definitely belongs in the same sentence with the terms *reward* and *punish*. We should change our vocabulary in business from "reward and punish" to "reward, punish, and condone," because many enterprises allow destructive behavior to continue by not dealing with it.

The U.S. Navy took a terrible blow to its reputation as an American institution as a result of the infamous Tailhook scandal. Incidents and reports of incidents of sexual harassment against women at a Las Vegas convention of Navy carrier pilots, ranging from verbal abuse to physical assault and near-rape, finally became too much for the organization to cover up. Journalists got the inside story and had a field day with it. When the responsible Navy brass tried to play down the incident and smooth it over, they offered a rationalization roughly along the lines of "boys will be boys." In other words, fighter pilots have always been hard-drinking, hard-partying young guys with an advanced case of testosterone poisoning. All they did was go a bit more over the line than they always do.

As the investigation tore into the organization, this line of defense turned out to be about the worst one anybody could have invented. Careers were ruined and even terminated, including those of an admiral and a number of other senior officers. In effect, the investigation concluded, the U.S. Navy had condoned, by silence, the ribald behavior and harassment of women that the code of conduct for officers presumably forbade. When the reckoning came, those who got caught in the crackdown felt double-crossed because they were now being punished for things that senior management had condoned for years.

It usually isn't very hard to decipher the rules of reward, punishment, and condonement in most organizations. But they aren't written on the wall; they're encoded in the folklore. Listen to the stories people tell about their successes and failures in working there. How do they describe the behavior of the executives? How do they interpret the politics of the organization? How did the various executives rise to the positions they occupy? Who are the people in the very inner circle, and what got them there? Are there any executive outcasts, and if so, what led to their banishment?

What kinds of assignments or opportunities are used as rewards? Are there others that serve as punishments or inducements to leave? Are certain fast-rising junior executives apparently anointed for stardom, and if so, why? Are there others widely regarded as going nowhere, and if so, why?

Are political empire building, infighting, turfism, and dishonesty condoned, or even encouraged? Does a person get ahead by contributing to the success of the enterprise, or by accumulating poker chips for his or her own account?

This is not to suggest that every organization has highly destructive politics, or that every one has a twisted system of reward, punishment, and condonement. But an honest appraisal of the culture is always in order. Nor is it always true that destructive reinforcement dynamics are the deliberate result of executive attitudes or actions. Some of the destructive forces that thwart, constrain, and discourage people in some enterprises are so embedded in their structures that nobody really causes them in any direct way.

In particular, think about the kinds of bureaucratic underbrush, restraints, controls, and barriers that grow up in highly structured organizations over the years. Government agencies in particular come to mind in this connection. In the worst of bureaucracies, there are formal systems that prevent people from acting on their own initiative and punish those who try to. These I refer to as organizational "chastity belts." They are elaborate systems of checking and cross-checking, approval levels, and reviews that completely thwart responsible action.

A typical form of the organizational chastity belt is the "sole-source justification" procedure, used when someone needs to purchase outside goods and services from a certain supplier selected without a process of formal competition. Ostensibly, this system ensures that managers will take advantage of competition among suppliers to get the best value for the funds they spend. In practical form, it typically slows down the process, wastes managerial time, and seldom improves the value received. If the objective is to get good value for our money, then displacing responsibility from the leadership of the enterprise to a mindless system is seldom a very good way to do it.

I'll offer a grotesque example of this "management by chastity belt." I was asked by an executive of a state government to make a presentation to a large annual governor's conference of all the state's senior managers. As the person responsible for organizing the conference, she had decided I was the person she wanted to deliver a message about the management of service. Although she was a very senior executive, and I was the only person in the world who presented this particular message, she still had to submit a sole-source justification package to some department that was supposed to make sure she didn't select the wrong speaker.

I had to spend time helping her prepare a formal explanation of why she had chosen this particular speaker to make the presentation to the governor and his executives. In addition, I had to fill out several forms and sign a notarized ten-page contract in connection with the assignment. At the conference, I opened the presentation with a comparison of their process with the more typical process by which business executives do the same thing for corporate conferences. Then I posed the question, Why doesn't this organization trust its leaders to lead?

Chastity belts don't make people chaste. At best—or worst—they may make it inconvenient for them to sin. But in the process they immobilize and disempower many trustworthy people, preventing them from creating the value they are capable of creating.

In the most arthritic of bureaucracies, it's more important not to be wrong than it is to be right. There is an insidious collusion of mediocrity at all levels, because the same system that ensures that nobody has the power to act also ensures that nobody will get blamed. Once there is enough ritual, procedure, and paperwork, no one person can be found guilty if something goes wrong. It's the fault of "the system." In even the most outrageous organizational blunder, somehow the executives are exonerated because they have been reduced to the role of presiders rather than leaders.

In his thought-provoking book *Corporate Dandelions*, Craig J. Cantoni analyzes creeping bureaucracy in terms of the metaphor of growing weeds:

> Over seventy years of brilliant management thinking have gone by since Max Weber defined bureaucracy. Why, then, are we still haunted by his ghost? Why are his tenets still practiced religiously? Why are corporations such stifling, bureaucratic, hierarchical places in which to work? . . .
>
> Through some sort of reverse Darwinian process, unfit bureaucrats have risen to the top floors of too many of the Fortune 500 companies, where they have given birth to large staffs and slow-moving bureaucracies. The bureaucratic offspring of such leaders are as abundant as dandelions in an unmowed field— even in this age of downsizing and cutbacks in white-collar workers.[4]

I don't recall who said it, but one of the most insightful statements ever made about bureaucracies is:

> You know that mediocrity is a way of life when the penalty for success gets to be as big as the reward for failure.

Are We a Team?

Have you ever had the experience of lying in a hospital bed, say after surgery or some medical procedure, and having a nurse realize just before sticking you with a syringe that he or she had the wrong medication? Gives you a nice, comfortable sense of confidence in the hospital, doesn't it? Is your sense of confidence improved when the nurse starts telling you how the pharmacy department can never get a medication right, and this is the fifth time this has happened this week?

As a customer, how do you feel when the airline ticket agent complains about the computer system? How do you feel when one department criticizes or blames another for the unsatisfactory treatment you're getting? How do you feel when two employees at different times give you exactly contradictory statements of the company's policy about a particular issue? One says there is a charge for the delivery, and the other says it's free. How do you feel about doing business with them?

The capacity for intelligent collective action is one of the biggest single advantages an enterprise can have in competing for the business of its customers. Yet far too many of them are more at war with themselves than capable of acting as a team.

For the people of your enterprise to work well as a team, both for the benefit of their customers and for the benefit of the enterprise itself, they require at least three things:

1. *Common purpose*—a shared understanding of the value the enterprise has pledged that they will create for their customers, the philosophy and business values that should guide the decisions they make, and a belief that everybody has a part to play in its success.

2. *Common knowledge*—a high level of individual job knowledge, as well as an understanding of how the overall organiza-

tion operates and what the customer goes through in the chain of events he or she experiences in getting a need met. Each person needs to see his or her contribution in the context of the overall process of creating value, not as just an isolated process to be repeated with a succession of faceless, standardized customers in the queue.

3. *Common sense*—the practical attitudes required to get things done regardless of the slipups, system malfunctions, and organizational quirks that might occasionally get in the way; the entitlement to act on one's own initiative, within reason; and the moral authority to solve customer problems rather than slavishly go by the book.

Every leadership team needs to look carefully at the organization through the eyes of its customers, and see what they see. They also need to look at the ability of its people to work together internally. Do the various internal-service departments actually treat the line departments as customers in their own right? Is there a sense of mutuality among departments, a sense of joint value creation and support to one another? While there is always a certain level of political interplay among units, is it in the realm of reasonably healthy interaction, given the normal amount of upward striving, career ambition, and competitiveness that usually exist in an organization?

In an organization of any significant size, the executives cannot create the future single-handedly. They must develop the enterprise into a constellation of teams within the overall team if they hope to bring the special talents and resources to bear on the challenge of creating superior customer value and sustaining a competitive advantage in the eyes of its customers.

Do We Learn and Develop?

Why do some organizations keep making the exact same mistakes over and over? Why do some repeatedly make the same blunders with their major customers and have to keep bribing them into coming back again? Why are there so many stupid (*stupid* defined as painful, costly, and at the same time easily preventable) mistakes going on in some organizations?

Why does the chief executive keep hiring one incompetent after another to fill a key position, seemingly unable to discern whether they have the capabilities needed before hiring them? Why do the same kinds of major projects always run into the exact same snags, with nobody seemingly able to see them coming?

If you hit yourself on the thumb with a hammer every time you undertake to drive a nail, either you're a self-abusing masochist or you have a learning disability. On a personal level, living life is like being enrolled in a series of courses you didn't choose and can't drop out of. If you don't learn the lesson being presented, whether it's about romance, marriage, career moves, making business deals, raising children, or about anything else, it eventually comes around again and you get to take the course over. A great deal of human frustration and misery involve flunking one or more of life's little courses and having to take it again. And the same applies to organizations.

Those organizations that can fix their mistakes only after they happen, and cannot figure out how not to make the same mistakes again, are forever caught at a primitive level of existence. In literal terms, they cannot learn. In his book *The Fifth Discipline*, Peter Senge advances the case for every enterprise's becoming a learning organization. He defines learning as "the expansion of one's capabilities to produce results."[5]

To say that an organization learns implies an ability on the part of its leaders and action people to discover the kinds of things it habitually bungles, to track down the failure mechanisms that cause those things to go wrong, and to redeploy knowledge, skills, and procedural tactics to make recurrence of the blunders less likely.

Learning, at least in organizations, seems to be hierarchical in nature. It proceeds in ascending levels. If you can't complete the learning process at one level, it is very difficult to tackle the one on the next level up. As Figure 6-1 illustrates, we can think of the *organizational learning hierarchy* as having five levels:

1. *Tasks.* A person who is doing the job properly is by definition "ready, willing, and able." He or she has (1) the tools and resources to do the work, (2) the attitude and desire to get it done, and (3) the specific skills and capacities to do it.

Figure 6-1.   How organizations learn, or fail to.

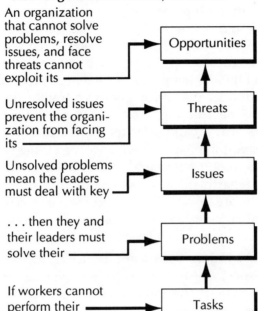

An organization that cannot solve problems, resolve issues, and face threats cannot exploit its ⟶ **Opportunities**

Unresolved issues prevent the organization from facing its ⟶ **Threats**

Unsolved problems mean the leaders must deal with key ⟶ **Issues**

. . . then they and their leaders must solve their ⟶ **Problems**

If workers cannot perform their ⟶ **Tasks**

If the person keeps having trouble doing the job effectively, then somebody has to look at the next level up, which is the problem level. The leader has to intervene to help the person, whether it is a "ready" problem, a "willing" problem, or an "able" problem.

2. *Problems.* A person who is not "ready" needs help in getting the proper tools, materials, and resources. One who is not "willing" needs to be confronted with the choice of either riding on the train or choosing a different train. And one who is not "able" needs either to get the training, preparation, and guidance to master the task or be reassigned to a new role that is within his or her capability to master. All three of these problem-solving actions are part of the job of the tactical unit leader. If the unit leader cannot or will not help the employee solve the problem, then somebody at the next level above the unit must deal with it, at the level of issues.

3. *Issues.* What blocks the employees and unit leaders from

solving their problems? Usually it is poor systems, procedures, and policies that keep two or more units from serving as a team. The design people can't finish the job without the right marketing information. The sales people can't promise the goods to the customer if the production people can't deliver. Nursing can't handle the patient's discharge proceedings properly if the physician's office doesn't provide the necessary information. The catering department can't serve the right refreshments at the banquet if the food and beverage people haven't ordered them, and "F&B" can't order the right refreshments unless they have accurate information from the people in the sales department who booked the function. On and on it goes. When organizational performance issues are standing in the way of solving the problems and performing the tasks, there are threats at the next level up the hierarchy.

4. *Threats.* Unless the organization can deal with its performance issues, solve the problems they cause, and free people to carry out the tasks that the problems have been blocking, the enterprise cannot deal with the threats to its success and perhaps eventually to its very survival. By definition, the ability to defeat the threats to survival involves the ability to change the organization's way of doing business. If it is so completely habit-driven, so arthritic in its processes, and so ignorant of the sources of its pain, it will continue to face the same lessons over and over again, without learning anything. And without the ability to face its threats, the organization cannot climb to the next higher level of the hierarchy and capitalize on its opportunities.

5. *Opportunities.* Going after new opportunities often requires that the organization learn some new ways of thinking, behaving, and deploying its talent. If it has demonstrated learning disabilities all the way up the hierarchy, what are the chances it can make the kinds of creative maneuvers to enter new markets, create value for new customers, cope with new competitors, and ride new shock waves? The question answers itself.

This notion of the learning organization starts out seeming a bit abstract, but it quickly takes on concrete meaning as you evaluate your own enterprise in this frame of reference. The objective of becoming a learning organization is not some fancy theoretical premise; it is the very essence of survival in turbulent business times. An important part of the organizational scan is to make a critical evaluation of the learning abilities and disabilities of your enterprise, and to determine what, if anything, it needs to learn to do better.

Are We Well Led?

What happens to an organization when the chief executive is incompetent to lead it? What happens when a number of the senior executives are either incompetent, inexperienced, misplaced, burned out, or otherwise incapable of leading the people in their domains of influence? Most books about creating "vision," setting strategy, planning direction, or whatever you choose to call it, seem to start with the polite assumption that the chief executive reading them has no hang-ups. They presume that this person, typically represented as a male, is psychologically mature, interpersonally skilled, level-headed, open-minded, conceptually fluent, logical, creative, open to new ideas, and comfortable with change. I've met very few chief executives that have all of those qualities in high measure. Most are normal human beings.

At the risk of alienating my primary audience, I feel compelled to raise the issue of executive competence as a fundamental factor in creating the northbound train and as a critical element of the enterprise's capability for getting the train out of the station. It is something we cannot afford to gloss over. Countless times I've had junior executives or high-level middle managers come to me in frustration and say of their chief, "You know, the problem is really Bob [or Carol, or Ted, or Alice]. He's lost. He doesn't really have the breadth of vision or the conceptual skills to lead us out of the mess we're in." Or they may feel the chief is not really committed to building an executive team, and that he prefers to play his own hand without letting anyone else know what cards he's holding.

What if the chief is an alcoholic, whose habit impairs his

ability to handle his role? What if his affair with a key female executive or junior employee has compromised his respect in the eyes of those whom he must lead? What if he is emotionally erratic, or even unstable? What if he is simply past his intellectual prime, unable or unwilling to tackle the new challenges of the day? What if he is just a few years from retirement and unwilling to rock his own boat, even though it's clear the boat is going nowhere? What if he is terminally stubborn or so intellectually arrogant that he cannot listen to the worldviews of others who have important insights to offer?

According to Thomas Horton, who spent twenty-eight years working in IBM and ten years as chairman of the American Management Association, chief executives are caught in an odd paradox, defined by the twin factors of seemingly limitless power and unrelenting accountability. In his book *The CEO Paradox*, Horton says:

> Underlying the issue of leadership are serious questions regarding privilege—and accountability. The chief executive of any organization is the person ultimately accountable for its success or failure. But to just whom, other than the organization's owners, *is* the CEO accountable, even to the owners?[6]

Executive competence is becoming a more important issue as the challenges to organizational survival become more complex. Traditionally, boards of directors have replaced chief executives only for retrospective reasons: They have fallen from political favor or alienated one or more powerful board members, or they must be sacrificed to appease the gods of Wall Street after a disastrous financial performance. But it is rather seldom that a board of directors considers carefully the challenges facing the enterprise and decides that the current chief executive is no longer the right person for the helm, especially if times have been good so far.

It is more common for an incoming chief executive to assess the capabilities of the existing leadership team and decide to replace some of them. This is something that probably should happen more often than it does.

A rarer, but more constructive, event is for the chief

executive and the others on the leadership team to honestly ask themselves, What new competencies must we acquire, as leaders and as a team, that are demanded by the new business reality our enterprise is facing? A related question is, What behaviors must we abandon, and what new ones must we adopt, if we are to provide the legitimate leadership needed by the people who are looking to us for the direction of the business?

Typically, leaders need some objective third party to help them gather some valid information about the effectiveness of their current behavior patterns, and about the kinds of leadership behavior needed by their people. Then they need to use their problem-solving skills to progress through the kinds of changes that are going to be necessary to meet the demands of their roles.

But we can't pick on just the chief and the senior executives in this part of the organizational scan. Leadership happens at all levels of the organization, and leaders at all levels must become accountable for the contributions required to turn the northbound train concept into a reality. An assessment of the total leadership strength of the organization is appropriate, on at least an annual basis. More and more organizations are using multilevel leadership assessment systems, in which each leader evaluates his or her own performance on a standard set of behaviors and gets comparative feedback about the evaluations of his or her team members and boss. This kind of assessment can provide invaluable insights to individual leaders, and it can give senior management a good profile of the overall leadership strength of the enterprise.

Are We Committed?

Any attempt at an organizational scan that does not address the "state of the heart," that is, the personal perceptions of the working people about being a part of the enterprise, is not a complete or valid picture. We need to understand what kinds of energy and commitment are available to the enterprise and what, if anything, may be standing in the way of releasing and focusing that energy and commitment.

Western management is in a state of confusion, and has been for some time, about what to do with the "employees." The new business imperatives make it more and more difficult to think in terms of managing employees, in the traditional sense of doing their thinking for them and telling them what to do. But many executives have not thought through their attitudes and beliefs about people, and many are not sure what approach they should take toward the workforce.

In truth, the Western management tradition seldom conceived of the people who do the work as critical or essential, or worthy of very much management attention. The latent, unexpressed view traditionally held that employees would always tolerate a certain amount of abuse and neglect, and, so long as they didn't launch a mutiny or call in a union to represent them, there was nothing in particular that management needed to do about them. The leaders of the company more or less "were" the company, in that they were relatively permanent, and the employees were something separate from the company, something like replaceable parts. "Turnover" was a concept applied to the workforce, not to management. When Western managers used the term *we*, the reference was usually to themselves as an identified in-group, not to the collective population of the organization.

Although Japanese management philosophy developed over several decades around the idea of capitalizing on the knowledge and commitment of the workers, Western management, and particularly American business-school philosophy, placed little emphasis on such matters. The worker was merely somebody who filled a slot and performed assigned tasks. Indeed, most of the efficiency and productivity methods developed by Americans tended to minimize the amount of worker know-how needed and made very little room for discretionary effort on the worker's part.

Now, the tremendous diversification of work, and the fact that more and more jobs involve using knowledge and skill to create value rather than just following preprogrammed tasks, means that managers must devote much more attention to the way people work, and, reluctantly in many cases, to the way they think and feel.

Some organizations have a long history of capitalizing on

the ideas and energy of their workers and paying attention to the quality of work life they experience. The Volvo Company of Sweden has for many years emphasized what its chairman, Pehr Gyllenhammar, calls the "invisible contract." In his words:

> Every person who works for Volvo has two kinds of contracts: one visible and one invisible. The visible one tells the formal terms of his or her employment, the pay, working conditions, and general job responsibilities. But it is the invisible contract that is the most important; this is the understanding between the worker as a person and Volvo as a company, about such things as commitment, feeling part of the team, the right to express one's views, the right to be treated fairly and with dignity, and a hope for a secure future.

John Foster, founder of the fast-growing medical services company NovaCare, states the case in similar terms. "The values of the organization," he maintains, "and the way a person has a right to be treated, represent the 'handshake,' so to speak, between NovaCare as an enterprise and the individual as a professional. People aren't employees of NovaCare; they *are* NovaCare."[7]

Yet it's striking how few organizations regularly measure and assess the state of the heart, the perceptions of quality of work life on the part of the people who work there. While some enterprises conduct annual surveys and follow-up group interviews with working-level people, many others do it on a haphazard, hit-or-miss basis, and many others don't do it at all.

Many organizations don't take advantage of the knowledge and insights to be gained from employee surveys because they don't know how to do them simply and efficiently. Typically, an organization that hasn't conducted an employee survey for five years or more will make a big, stressful project out of it. They will form task forces, get bids from consulting firms, and spend many meetings just designing the survey questionnaire. Each executive insists on including his or her particular pet questions, until the questionnaire becomes unwieldy with a hundred items or more. Then they go through a big uproar administering the thing and persuading people to fill it out. Next they hire a survey firm to process all the data and prepare a suitably large and impressive report, which very few executives or managers ever actually read.

If the results are alarmingly negative, the executives may suppress the report and hope the whole thing will fade away, but the employees are certain to be asking, "Are you going to show us the results of what we said on the survey?" When the whole thing is rat-holed, more damage than good has been done. In any case, most companies that go through this overkill on a quality-of-work-life survey don't have the stomach to face one again for another five years or more. Consequently, they have no simple baseline variables that could help them track employee perceptions over time.

Instead of a monstrous project and a snoozer of a report that few people read, most organizations should start with a fairly simple baseline survey, say twenty to fifty question items at most. This makes the project manageable, gives results that are digestible and meaningful, and makes it easy to use the survey on an annual or semiannual basis to provide important management information about the culture of the enterprise. Some firms actually spread the survey out over a whole year, for example by contacting 25 percent of the people every quarter, so the data are more recent while the logistics of gathering them are still manageable.[8]

This kind of perceptual information, representing the vital signs of the culture, can be just as important and valuable as market data, performance data, or environmental trends. It deserves the same serious treatment in gathering it and thinking about it that is accorded the other sources of information the leaders use in running the business.

In all of the elements of the organizational scan discussed above, it is important to maintain an element of objectivity. In some cases, the senior leaders of the enterprise may feel they are able to appraise the organization without filtering the truth through their own personal biases. In others, they may decide to seek outside help. Whatever the approach, it is important that the organizational scan provide a realistic basis for deciding which of the apparent opportunities are real ones, based on what the organization is really capable of doing.

Notes

1. Thomas J. Peters and Robert H. Waterman, *In Search of Excellence: Lessons from America's Best-Run Companies* (New York: Harper & Row, 1982), preface.
2. Deborah Tannen, *You Just Don't Understand* (New York: Simon and Schuster, 1991). Also available on audiotape from Simon and Schuster's audio products division.
3. There are various assessment instruments that give profiles of thinking styles and personality patterns. The most widely used of these are the Myers-Briggs Type Indicator, The Hermann Brain Dominance Instrument, and Karl Albrecht's Mindex Thinking Styles Profile. The first two are available through Pfeiffer & Associates in San Diego (formerly University Associates). The latter is available from Karl Albrecht & Associates, also in San Diego.
4. Craig T. Cantoni, *Corporate Dandelions: How the Weed of Bureaucracy Is Choking American Companies—And What You Can Do to Uproot It* (New York: AMACOM, 1993), pp. 5, 19.
5. Peter Senge, *The Fifth Discipline: The Art and Science of the Learning Organization* (New York: Doubleday, 1990).
6. Thomas R. Horton, *The CEO Paradox: The Privilege and Accountability of Leadership* (New York: AMACOM, 1992), p. xvii.
7. Speech given to NovaCare management.
8. There are now a number of effective PC software products available for creating and processing survey questionnaires easily and efficiently. Some require extensive statistical knowledge, while others are much simpler. The simplest of these is SurveyMaker (published by Karl Albrecht & Associates in San Diego).

Chapter 7

The Opportunity Scan: What Are Our Possibilities?

Who the hell wants to hear actors talk?

Harry M. Warner, Warner Brothers Pictures, 1927

Bifocal Vision: The Near Field and the Far Field

When the Apollo 7 astronauts left the Earth in their spaceship on their voyage to the moon, they didn't aim the rocket at the moon. They aimed it at the place where the moon was going to be, allowing for the time needed to get there. This is a crucial point of strategy thinking; we must act in advance of the critical changes going on in the environment if we are to succeed.

All-star hockey player Wayne Gretzky offered a similar analogy to this anticipatory thinking. He said, "When I skate into the action, I don't skate to where the puck is; I skate to where I think it's going to be, and that makes all the difference." It's this instinct for the next play that makes the difference between the *reactors* and the *proactors*. Proactors act from a sense of process, a conception of what *will* happen, not merely what *is* happening.

Bob Galvin, ex-CEO of Motorola Corporation, believes that

leaders should be evaluated on the twin skills of *anticipation* and *commitment*. Says Galvin, "Today's leaders must both anticipate the big opportunities of the future, and commit their organizations to doing what it takes to exploit them. We need to evaluate the track records of our leaders over the long run in these terms."

Every leader needs *bifocal vision*—the ability to perceive accurately things happening further out toward the horizon that will inevitably affect the enterprise, as well as the ability to focus on the more immediate, pressing events in its environment. This ability to see the far field as well as the near field, and to deal comfortably with both, is relatively rare. Indeed, it is often not an easy thing to do, even for the brightest of people.

For instance, what should you as a leader do if your view of the far field tells you that continuing to do business as you have will eventually bring disaster? What if your organization's success model for today is the failure model for tomorrow? At what point do you face that news? At what point do you start to get serious about changing the model?

Suppose you're in the car-making business. Suppose your current success model concentrates on making cars more stylish, more fuel-efficient, and more feature-rich. Suppose also, however, that your view of the future tells you that the internal-combustion engine must be abandoned. With major cities like Mexico City choking in polluted air to the extent that automobile use must be rationed, and other cities not far behind, the gasoline-operated automobile may very soon be the wrong solution. We may even come to a world one day in which the individual transportation unit will be obsolete. But if your firm has spent fifty years or more perfecting its version of the gasoline-run car, and you as an executive have built your career on doing that well, at what point will you begin thinking seriously about giving it up and committing to something else?

Many IBM-watchers believe the company's business problems stem from faulty bifocal vision. As the personal computer phenomenon spread throughout businesses worldwide, and as PC prices kept dropping dramatically, the way organizations processed data began to change. Meanwhile, IBM's leaders focused their attention on the mainframe market, which was the company's traditional cash-cow product line. The wide availability of cheap computing power in small machines led managers to set up their own miniature computer departments. Then, the idea of networking all of these tiny computers into a collective distributed "organizational brain" began to change the paradigm of data processing.

After all, the only reason managers ever sent their data to the computer department to have it processed was that the machines that did the job were so big and expensive the company could only afford to buy one of them. Once every manager could have his or her own computer, and once commercial software products rapidly surpassed the klunky mainframe versions in versatility and flexibility, the high priests of the internal computer departments had to rethink their roles. While IBM's leaders continued to ride the mainframe as their favored horse, the rise of such billion-dollar PC makers as Apple, Compaq, Dell, and others, and software firms such as Microsoft, Lotus, Ashton-Tate, and Borland, created the marketing power to make the PC a force in its own right.

Some computer experts predict that the mainframe computer will eventually disappear as computing becomes fully distributed and networked throughout organizations, and as computing and communicating merge into a unified information technology. At best, they feel, the mainframe will have to be downsized from the typical million-dollar price tag to something below the hundred-thousand-dollar level. Even at that, it may be relegated to certain special-purpose applications that require dedicated processing.

Yet when Louis Gerstner took over the helm of IBM in the aftermath of CEO John Akers's departure, one of his first pronouncements at a meeting of senior managers was, "The last thing IBM needs is a vision." Presumably he meant that the people in the company simply had to try harder, focus more carefully on results, and get the day's work done. While that is always a requirement, concentrating harder on the near field may not do much to change the prospect of the far field.

Contrast Gerstner's disdain for visioning with the simple but compelling corporate philosophy of Microsoft. According to Microsoft's founder and chairman, Bill Gates, that company has built its whole concept—its northbound train—on the far field. "Our vision," says Gates, "is very simple. It's a computer on every desk and in every home, running Microsoft software."

Corposaurus: Dinosaur Thinking Can Lead to Extinction

Some scientists believe that large dinosaurs had such primitive nervous systems that, if something bit a dinosaur on the tail, the nerve signal could take five seconds or more to reach its brain. If true, that would seem to be a serious handicap for the dinosaur. Yet many business organizations have somewhat the same kinds of reaction times when it comes to making major responses to the shock waves and major trends in their environments.

Organizational inertia can be incredibly powerful, and more than one business has hit the rocks because it couldn't muster an appropriate reaction to a major threat. Government organizations in particular tend to exhibit this same paralysis in the face of approaching crisis. During the Persian Gulf War in 1992, for example, the Japanese government was severely criticized by other countries for its slow response to the immediate crisis and to the need to build up the logistical resources for the effort. Their response of simply providing funds was derided as "checkbook diplomacy." However, their response was in fact slow and inappropriate largely because their arthritic, consensus-bound governmental mechanisms just couldn't make decisions quickly.

For some businesses, it may not be a problem of being unable to embrace the future so much as being unable to abandon the past and even the present. Management consultant and author Peter Drucker frequently counsels executives to practice "planned abandonment." "Make a list," says Drucker, "of all the things you are doing today that, if you were not already doing, you would not be willing to start doing. These are your candidates for abandonment."

Virtually all business organizations are saddled with one or more commitments, processes, investments, structures, or policies that do not serve their interests well. Yet abandoning them is often difficult because they are woven into the psyche of the culture and they have become so fossilized that no one thinks of them as options anymore.

The difficult truth is that we human beings are not good at abandoning things. Most homes have at least a closetful of stuff that nobody needs, wants, or uses, and yet we can't bear to throw it away. Organizations have their own figurative junk closets, too.

Letting go of the known in exchange for a commitment to the unknown is not something most human beings do comfortably or well. Even in major disasters such as impending hurricanes or floods, people will cling to their homes. In many cases, police must literally drive people from their houses in order to save their lives. And organizations, or more precisely people operating in organizations, have the same attachments to the known.

Organizations tend to react to an immediate crisis, an impending crisis, or the possibility of a crisis in fairly predictable ways. It is a rare enterprise whose leaders have enabled it to get ahead of events and capitalize on major changes. Almost anyone can react to an absolutely undeniable crisis, such as a sudden drop in sales, the total collapse of a market sector, a major product liability problem, or an employee mutiny. But reacting to a *possible crisis* is something else. In a state of ambiguity, a problem that could well turn into a crisis if not handled well can get temporarily swept under the carpet.

This tends to be the classic case with almost any corporation that has protected monopoly status in its industry, much as AT&T had before its breakup and the extensive deregulation of the American telecommunications industry. Nationally owned companies in the United Kingdom, Canada, Australia, and similar quasi-socialist economies have faced very difficult adjustments when they have been privatized or deprived of full protection. After decades of believing they had a God-given right to abuse their customers, many have faced a painful comeuppance when the newly empowered customers have risen up in righteous wrath.

Telecom Australia went through a predictably slow period of adjustment as its customers learned they have new options. Newly started Optus Communications, a joint venture between Australian and American companies, opened its doors with a respectable chunk of the market, largely on the strength of the "revenge" response. Many Australian customers, having endured decades of what they perceived as neglect and abuse bordering on sheer arrogance, jumped at the chance to punish Telecom by giving their business to Optus, without knowing or even caring whether they would get better treatment or better prices.

Having worked with Telecom's senior management several years earlier, I could see that the organization was very unlikely to mount a strong defense against the incursion of new competitors, especially small firms that aggressively targeted specific parts of the business. The company's leaders had wrung their hands and rolled their eyes for many months in advance of the expected deregulation but were unable to develop a sense of urgency appropriate to the threats that faced them.

One of the junior executives of the company recently told me: "It's very much like what Henry Kissinger had to say when he came back from one of his Middle East peacemaking trips and reported that the Israelis and their Arab enemies weren't ready to make peace. He said, 'More people have to die.' And that's us. We won't really react effectively until we see our own blood being spilled."

Reaction patterns in organizations tend to be much the same for isolated emergencies as for major strategic challenges. Leaders who tend to bungle an acute, isolated crisis or emergency also tend to bungle the more complex strategic problems. If they are fuzzy in their thinking about the tactical problems, they will tend to be fuzzy about the big ones. If they take too long in reacting to one, they will likely take a long time in reacting to the other.

How well an organization reacts to a potential strategic crisis or a clearly tactical problem depends on the ability of its leaders to:

- See it clearly, that is, identify the clues that suggest something may be going wrong.
- Interpret the clues effectively and make a realistic assessment of what is likely to happen if the organization doesn't act effectively.

- Mobilize the concern and energies of those in the organization who must be part of the response.
- Make decisions and commit energies to a definitive course of action.

The daily news is full of reports about organizations that fail to face short-term tactical crises only to see them blow up into raw material for the media. Accusations of bribing of government officials are stoutly denied until the evidence becomes overwhelming. Then the organization's leaders find themselves in a defensive, no-win situation trying to minimize the damage.

A rape on a college campus is hushed up by the administration, but it gets into the news anyway. Now the reporters have a field day with the cover-up, which does more damage to the institution's image than would have been done if the incident had been dealt with honestly and openly.

A whistle-blower in a government procurement office is demoted, harassed, and intimidated into silence in hopes that things won't get out of hand. When they do, and the crisis becomes a major one, there aren't too many attractive options.

"Corposaurus," the quintessential dinosaurlike organization, typically reacts to untidy problems in a distinct pattern of defensiveness:

1. *Denial*. The leaders refuse to accept that there is a problem; those who claim there is are criticized, ridiculed, branded pessimists, accused of being disloyal, or even ostracized from the inner circles of decision making. There is collusion, often unconscious, that says, "If we don't think about it or talk about it, maybe it will go away; or maybe it won't be too bad."

2. *Rationalizing*. When the problem becomes so apparent that it can no longer be denied, the view is, "Well, yes, there is a problem, but. . . ." At this point the focus shifts to fixing blame for the problem on somebody else, explaining why there is nothing that can be done about the problem, or proving nothing needs to be done "right now."

3. *Acceptance*. When the problem causes undeniable pain and immediate discomfort, people begin making whatever

obvious responses they can think of. These are typically defensive moves, like putting out press releases, declaring press blackouts, calling in the attorneys, and sacrificial firings in hopes of appeasing their attackers. With luck, they may begin to acknowledge the seriousness of the problem and begin trying to understand it fully.

4. *Problem solving.* This is the stage of full commitment to solving the problem in whatever ways seem most effective. It brings a willingness to do things differently, to stop doing the unproductive or destructive things that stand in the way of solving the problem, and to rethink some basic attitudes.

5. *Learning and growing.* Sometimes a bungled disaster helps people in the organization learn how to face their problems more honestly and effectively. In the agonizing that follows a painful episode, people may increase their willingness to face difficult problems rather than avoid them, and they may come to understand that trying to make a problem go away only makes the eventual solution much more painful.

The key point about bifocal vision and dinosaurian reactions is that the enterprise can be its own worst enemy if it does not have the leadership, insight, and honest willingness to face, solve, and adjust to the challenges presented to it by its environment.

Opportunities and Threats

One of the time-worn but still effective steps in strategy thinking is the SWOT analysis, which stands for strengths, weaknesses, opportunities, and threats. In our approach, we have looked at strengths and weaknesses under the organizational scan. Under the opportunity scan, we look at opportunities and threats.

Bear in mind that the same event or trend can represent both a threat and an opportunity. The way you respond to it and how well your response works out puts it either on the "win" side of the scorecard or the "loss" side. In working through the opportunity scan, it helps to think carefully about what it takes to discern an opportunity or a threat. What do they look like through the window of strategy thinking?

In order to make the following discussion broad enough to apply to as many different types of business as possible, it will be helpful to use a newer term in place of the traditional phrase *product or service*. The term *product* is too narrow, and the term *service* leaves people in some industries feeling left out. For this discussion and the remainder of the book, I shall use the more encompassing term *value package* to describe an enterprise's basic competitive offering. Your value package consists of everything you provide, either tangible or intangible, directly or indirectly, that meets customer needs. In effect, the value package is unique for each industry and each enterprise.

Opportunities are created mostly by events, trends, or possibilities for action that promise to:

• *Expand the size of your customer base*—natural growth in the number of customers, due to any of a variety of changes, such as demographic shifts in the population, rising incomes or improving economic conditions that release more disposable income, a significant increase in customer behavior such as outsourcing, and increasing threats or opportunities to your customers that push them in the direction of needing what you can offer.

• *Give you new avenues for customer access*—new ways of packaging products or bundling services that reach the same customers with an expanded selling proposition, new channels for advertising or delivery as a result of alliances or coventures, and creation of "customer access products" specifically crafted to maintain continuous contact so you can reduce selling costs for repeat sales.

• *Increase the customer appeal of your value package* compared to those of competitors for the customer's trade. This can involve more than beating out the competitor; it can involve enticing the customer to choose your value package over alternative ways of meeting his or her need, not just preferring your offering over similar ones.

• *Exploit a weakness or a blunder by a competitor*. A competitor who is heavily committed psychologically and financially to an unpromising strategic avenue may take longer than otherwise to respond to a fresh initiative on your part. You may have a window of opportunity for running unopposed, during which time you can build customer acceptance of your approach.

Threats are created mostly by events, trends, or competitor actions that can:

• *Reduce the size of your customer base.* This includes demographic shifts, for example, that cause some customers to move out of your category, outgrow the age range of primary demand, or change to lifestyles that focus on alternative means for meeting their needs. Sometimes your customers become your competitors. An example of this is insourcing, in which the customer acquires the capability for doing something traditionally outsourced, perhaps because new technology has made the process much less expensive.

• *Make customer access more difficult or more costly*—changes in customer buying practices, such as doing business with a smaller number of preferred suppliers, directing their business through agents or third parties, greater use of formal competitions, and reduction of product ranges by choosing distributors who prefer to order from only a few suppliers.

• *Reduce the customer appeal of your primary value package* compared to other choices the customer may have for solving his or her problem. Price wars in one discretionary industry, such as air travel, for example, can siphon off demand in another such industry, such as local leisure activities.

• *Surpass or eclipse your value package*—a new or greatly improved offering on the part of a competing provider, a nightmare justifiably feared by every marketing executive. This might include vicious price cutting, technological leapfrogging, or refocusing the value package at a significantly higher or lower price point.

These are just some starting ideas, intended to reinforce the need for a careful, thorough, wide-ranging, and realistic appraisal of the happenings in the environment that represent threats to be faced and opportunities to be exploited.

Vulnerable Industries: Dinosaur Herds?

In some cases, whole industries are threatened by changes so fundamental they can change the rules of the game. It's easy to identify some industries, especially in the industrialized Western countries, that could face near-extinction or severe restructuring of their worlds. Some of the most noticeable ones are:

• *Banking.* A very traditional industry to which change and innovation come slowly and painfully, banking is profoundly threatened by new technological options. For centuries, most banks have been in the business of warehousing money and lending some of it out from the warehouse. But money itself has changed profoundly, especially during the last two decades.

Gold was the original favorite as a form of money because of its scarcity and its use as a store of value. With fractional-reserve banking, money turned into paper; no advanced country now exchanges its currency directly for gold anymore. With the age of electronics and telecommunications, money has now become electronic. Most wage earners never see most of their money: It exists as binary digits inside computers. Electronic money can now travel about, literally across the world, at astonishing speeds. This means that banks, if they are to survive, must redefine themselves. They are not in the business of warehousing money; they are in the information business.

The leaders of banks will have to realize, and very quickly, that they are simply participants in the skillful handling of the value-based information that forms part of the economic life of modern-day customers. Banks have virtually no protective barriers any longer against potential outside competitors who want to serve the same needs they do. Indeed, the heavy concentration on traditional brick-and-mortar branch operations makes most large banks uncomfortably dependent on expensive real estate.

Brokerage firms and other broad-scale financial service companies are steadily encroaching, to the extent that the basic definition of banking is becoming confused. Practically speaking, any telephone company or similar operation with a modest amount of capital and a good computer system could do just about anything a typical bank can do. The corner branch bank may not be the model for the future. Unfortunately, many banks, perhaps most, are not yet dealing with this fundamental threat proposition.

• *Publishing.* "Print," as a medium of communication in Western countries, and particularly the United States, has been declared dead by many who see the all-pervasive audiovisual culture as undermining reliance on the written word. The epitaph is probably a bit premature, but the concern is certainly a legitimate one. Educated, literate people who walk into bookstores and marvel at the wealth of interesting and useful knowledge on sale there typically don't realize that they are a very small minority of citizens. Publishers estimate that about 5 to 10 percent of the population are readers, meaning people who regularly read a few books per month. If you subtract out those who read escape fiction, such as adventures, mysteries, and gothic novels, you probably have a core of heavy nonfiction readers of about 5 percent of the population.

The typical citizen is substantially out of touch with the kind of serious discourse provided by literature. A very large fraction of adults in countries like America are literate only to the point of being able to function with written material, but they are certainly not comfortable in picking up a serious magazine article or book dealing with a complex subject of current importance.

Television is indeed the primary source of "information" for the typical Western citizen. And the very nature of television, functioning as it does in an entertainment format, guarantees that information density will be sacrificed to emotional immediacy. No serious student of national issues could expect to rely on television coverage to glean enough information to form an intelligent perspective on a particular topic. That is not typically the function of television, except for certain "public broadcast" programs, whose share of viewership approximates the proportion of people who read books.

To the extent that television competes with books for a person's time and attention, it seems evident that the book-publishing industry will have difficulty growing, or even holding its own. And given the increasing demands on the time of business professionals, who tend to be strong consumers of books, even they have less and less time to devote to reading conventionally designed books. Nonfiction books such as business books are getting shorter, physically smaller, more topic-focused, and more condensed.

Traditional print publishers who want to stay alive and well in this new information environment will have to learn to think in new ways. They will have to redefine themselves as being in the business of selling information products, not the business of publishing books. And they will have to start to understand and exploit the various alternatives to ink, such as video, computer software, on-line information services, and innovative information packaging as ways to serve customer needs.

• *Public education.* In most Western countries, publicly funded and managed schools are far short of their potential for the roles they should be playing. The availability of remarkable new options for imparting information interactively and individually, such as video, computers, and interactive compact discs, currently poses more of a perceived threat to traditional schools and traditional teachers than an opportunity. The lack of any competitive performance pressures on public schools has kept most of them from using computers for anything other than occasionally keeping kids amused and giving teachers a rest. The opportunity is to profoundly rethink the entire educational experience, breaking the lockstep system of yearly tracks and fifty-minute sessions that serve no other purpose than to be convenient for teachers and administrators. Education could actually become an engaging, stimulating, exciting, and rewarding experience. Children from disadvantaged homes would probably benefit, proportionately, most of all.

As more and more government bodies explore the option of customer choice, for example, allowing families to choose their own schools and to allocate funds through vouchers they "spend" with the schools they choose, technology will enable private schools to deliver a superior educational experience at lower cost. This will put enormous pressure on traditional public schools to improve. Currently, teachers' unions in the United States are fighting this trend with all their might, but in the end they will lose. The issue is quality, and technology supplies most of the answers.

Colleges and universities may not be far behind the primary and secondary schools, in terms of the beating they could take from a newly developing competitive industry. They have been traditionally protected from competition by government policies, politically oriented accreditation systems, and an attitude of condescension and intimidation toward their students, who have not traditionally thought of themselves as customers. Technology will surely make available competitive options to the standard four-year "paper chase" and will open up educational opportunities to people who can't sacrifice four years of earnings to pursue a degree.

In addition, large employers are progressively becoming the educators of last resort, making up for the weakness in primary and secondary schools and for the lack of relevance of much of the university education people bring to work. None of these trends bode well for the comfortable role our educational institutions have enjoyed for over one hundred years.

• *Law enforcement.* In America more than most developed countries, but increasingly in all of them, traditional police organizations are more and more seen as helpless and limited to handling only acute episodes of crime. Public safety has become virtually a lost cause in the minds of most citizens. With the traditional bureaucratic, civil service mentality inhibiting most municipal police organizations from any serious attack on the problems of lawlessness, we will certainly see an increase in community activism, a rise in private crime prevention services, and a greater investment by businesses and private citizens in security systems and services.

Unfortunately for them, most police organizations can't actually go out of business, because of their historical mandate to chase criminals. But the possibilities they might otherwise enjoy, in terms of building themselves into major enterprises dedicated to public safety, will probably always elude most of them. Those few that can really redefine themselves and focus their energies on creating value rather than on arriving after the crime is committed, could enjoy unprecedented public support and access to resources.

Other industries face similar kinds of threats. Newspaper publishers, for example, face many of the same kinds of threats faced by book publishers, but with different economic variables. As advertising customers get lured by other media, and as fewer people rely on print journalism for their worldviews, newspapers are increasingly having to struggle to remain viable. More and more of them will probably fail, and many of them will have to diversify their approaches.

Even traditional institutions such as churches face problems retaining their "customers." A recent *Wall Street Journal* article reported that the Ursuline order of nuns, based in Youngstown, Ohio, engaged an advertising/PR firm in Cincinnati to help get its message across to potential nuns. Having seen a 50 percent drop in new candidates, and a nationwide drop of nearly that much in the ranks of nuns, they decided to craft a modernized message to their marketplace.[1]

Scenario Planning: Playing the Possible Futures

In some cases, the environment presents a quandary. What to do if the fate of your enterprise could rise or fall dramatically based on some impending event beyond your control? What if there are two or more possible forks in the road, and you don't know which way they will turn? For example, will a trade war between your country and another result in tariffs that devastate the market for your product? Will your major customer go into bankruptcy and cease buying from you? Will you win the largest contract in your company's history, or not? Which way will the litigation go between the two biggest operators in your industry, and how will it affect your right to do business? Will a major change in a crucial government program wipe out part of your industry, or revitalize it? Will your organization be closed down or merged with another, or will it continue to exist?

How can you hope to develop a sensible strategic approach

in the face of such fundamental uncertainty? Do you just abandon the strategy process and wait to see what happens? You could, but what if it will take several years for the uncertainty to be resolved? Can you afford to drift along with no clear direction? Will some of your best options be invalid by that time? Will your competitors have strengthened their positions? Will the ones who gamble on a particular outcome have the advantage if they happen to pick the right one?

In situations like this, sophisticated strategists turn to *scenario planning*, which, in its various forms, is a way to work out broad options for uncontrollable outcomes and develop an attack plan for each one. This doesn't have to be an extremely elaborate or complex process, although some organizations choose to make it so. The germ of the idea is fairly simple; it's up to the leaders to make it work best for their enterprise.

The basic approach of scenario planning was developed in the 1970s, most notably by Royal Dutch Shell in Europe. The company faced difficult questions associated with worldwide patterns of demand and opportunity for its products. Shell's strategy thinkers began to look at world business in terms of the "Triad," that is, North America, Japan, and Western Europe. In their view, the primary world economy consists of the Triad countries, which accounts for two thirds of the world's income with only 15 percent of the world's people. The rest of the countries are so economically retarded as to fall into the "miscellaneous" category.

Proceeding from this definition of the playing field, Shell strategists tried to sketch out the major scenarios they believed would be created by the actions of the major players such as the United States, Japan, the European Community, and the Soviet Union. The primary role of the USSR at that time, before its collapse and the worldwide fall of communism, was not as an economic power but as an antagonist to the United States; its Cold War initiatives would strongly influence American economic strategies. Then, by sorting out the few key options for the behavior of the principal "actors," they derived several scenarios.

One key scenario variable was whether America and the USSR would either intensify the Cold War or achieve some significant détente. Matched against this variable was whether

America and Japan would either engage in a destructive trade war or find a comfortable basis for doing business together.

Anglo American Corporation's strategy expert, Clem Sunter, examined these same variables in trying to sketch out possible futures for the South African firm's operations. In his book *The World and South Africa in the 1990s,* Sunter constructed four primary scenarios out of the two variables and the two choices for each, as illustrated in Figure 7-1.[2] (I have adapted his original captions to suit the point of this discussion.)

By combining the two variables on a grid diagram, Sunter showed the four alternative futures Anglo-American and its competitors could be facing:

1. *Dual wars*—the United States would be in both an escalated cold war with the USSR and a vicious trade war with Japan. This would be the worst scenario in terms of growth in the Triad economies, investment in research and development, transfer of technology, and opening up of world markets. Japanese companies would have the significant advantage collectively, because a very small portion of the country's income

Figure 7-1.   An example of scenario planning.

	Trade peace	Imperial Twilight	Industrial Renaissance
U.S. and Japan	Trade war	Dual Wars	Protracted Transition
		Cold War	Détente

U.S. and Russia

goes to military expenditures, while much of America's wealth and talent would be diverted to non–value-creating output such as weapons and munitions. The continued international tensions would certainly have a dampening effect on alliances across national borders.

2. *Protracted transition*—détente between the United States and the USSR, but with trade war between the United States and Japan. The United States could redirect its resources toward economic development, but the trade barriers would inhibit the speed of technology transfer and sharing of innovations, probably between Japan and Europe as well. Import and export restrictions would hold down economic growth for both countries by inhibiting demand and restraining trade.

3. *Imperial twilight*—continuation of the arms race, but with cooperation between the United States and Japan. This would be an in-between scenario, in which both countries could cooperate economically and technologically, but in which the United States would continue to have to waste resources on the military buildup.

4. *Industrial renaissance*—the best of the four scenarios, with the Cold War easing and the trade war averted. This would create freer markets, better trade and technological cooperation, and accelerated development of technology because of increased investment and redirection of talent and scientific resources toward commercial ends.

The essence of scenario planning is not in trying to predict the future, which recent history has shown to be futile, but in discovering the most likely variations among alternative possible futures. You can first do an environmental scan for each of the scenarios as if it were the only one. Then you can compare them to see what elements they have in common, as well as what threats and opportunities they all present. This thinking process can build a basis for a flexible strategic direction that can minimize the risks of being wrong and maximize the possible benefits of circumstances as they actually unfold.

The previous scenarios may or may not relate directly to your current business environment, but presumably the basic ideas are clear. You need to do five things:

1. *Build the "stage."* Form a concept of the arena in which the action will take place. How do you choose to model your strategic environment: as a global economy, one particular business sector, a regulated industry, a field of fast-moving technology, or some other dynamic construct? It is crucial to get consensus about the conceptual framework for the scenario analysis. This clarity should come from careful thinking about the basic uncertainties that led you to a scenario approach in the first place.

2. *Cast the key actors.* These are the big players whose actions have big side effects or direct consequences for your enterprise and others that compete with you. Are they nations, national governments, legislatures, political parties or groups, large government agencies, dominant corporations in your industry, suppliers of capital, owners or developers of critical technology, or even journalists and media producers whose outputs shape public opinion?

3. *Script the alternative roles for the actors.* What are the two or three major variations in behavior that each of the actors or "interactors" could exhibit? How many combinations of variations are there, and which ones deserve primary attention? Keep this to a manageable number, not only for conceptual simplicity but to focus on the most significant consequences that might occur.

4. *Lay out the key scenarios.* A scenario is one particular combination of actors and actions that creates a distinct business reality. Make an environmental scan and an opportunity scan of each scenario and put the results into some kind of graphic picture or other useful comparative form. This includes identifying any shock waves, critical trends, and potentially critical events you need to deal with.

5. *Find the common strategic themes.* What organizational capability must you have that is common to dealing with all of the major scenarios? What kinds of customer access, what kinds of technological solutions, what kinds of alliances and partnerships are in the cards regardless of which scenario actually unfolds?

This kind of analysis can be invaluable as input to an executive strategy retreat. Even better, if possible, is having the executives themselves work through the formation of scenarios. They are likely to use the approach much more effectively if they personally develop the scenario model.

What's Hot and What's Not: Modeling the Market

Just about all of the thinking processes presented so far have the benefit of simplifying complex information and ideas, and putting them into a useful framework for intelligent discussion. We need to do the same thing for the complicated interplay of customers, value packages, and competitors. We need some simple models that can quickly portray some of the most important realities of the business environment so the leaders of the enterprise can think about them effectively.

Strategy thinkers often use simple matrix charts to portray relationships between customers and products, customers and competing suppliers, and products and suppliers. Three of these classical models deserve mention here:

1. *The niche matrix.* As illustrated by the hypothetical example in Figure 7-2, you can array the range of potential customers on one axis and the range of value-package options you're considering on the other. This makes a checkerboard grid of combinations of customer and value package. The trick in getting value from this model is in identifying the categories you want to use in classifying customers and value packages. For the customer axis, it might be appropriate in one case to arrange them by age; in yet another, income levels might be more significant; in others, life stages may be better.

For the value-package axis, one case might call for organizing them according to their defining features; in another case, price range might be more relevant; in yet another, the means for getting the item to the customer might be more significant. In such a diagram there will usually be squares that don't make feasible combinations. Preteens would not be candidates to buy cars, but they might match up well with bicycles. Young marrieds might not buy many boats, but mature professionals might.

A feasible combination of a customer type and a value-package type defines a *niche*, in market-research terms. How-

Figure 7-2.   The niche matrix.

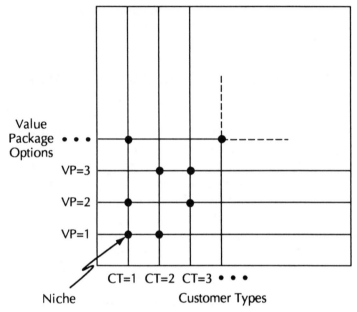

ever, even if a certain niche is feasible, it's another matter to find out if it offers real buying power. Is it a "rich niche"? The value of the niche matrix is in giving you a complete taxonomy of options to consider, both in terms of customers and the range of value packages. This is especially important in a fast-changing environment where there are new value-package ideas emerging and new customer profiles. Based on that information, the leadership team can evaluate all of the interesting niches and look for patterns that can create synergy in aspects such as customer access, continuity of marketing, and business alliances.

2. *The life-cycle matrix.* Appearing over the years in various forms with various names, this diagram illustrates, as shown in Figure 7-3, where your products or value packages are in the cradle-to-grave life-cycle stages of growth, plateau, and decline. Heavily promoted by the Boston Consulting Group as well as others, this approach shows the market demand for the value package on one axis and the competitive strength of your particular version on the other axis. BCG popularized colorful

Figure 7-3. The life-cycle matrix.

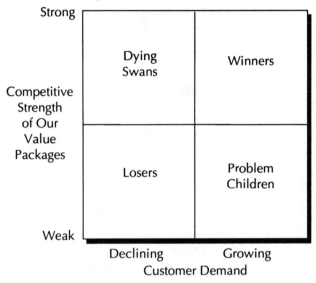

nicknames for the four categories: (1) "dogs," which are weak products in dying demand phases, (2) "marginals," which are weak products in growth markets, (3) "cash cows," which are strong products in their declining phases, and (4) "stars," which are the ideal combinations of strong products in advancing markets. I prefer slightly different names, but the general concept is virtually the same.

While this kind of analysis can be a bit oversimplified, it does help the leaders of an enterprise to face the facts of its existence. Again, the value of this kind of review can depend greatly on the validity of the ranking information. If the review is based solidly on customer perception, it is more likely to lead to effective decisions than if it is just the "wet finger in the wind" kind of research.

3. *The competitive matrix.* As Figure 7-4 shows, it is often useful to compare the appeal of your value package in the eyes of the customer to those of your competitors. By plotting a range of customer-value attributes on one scale and the relative standing of you and your competitors aligned with it on the other scale, you can get a better perspective on the customer's choices for a particular value package.

Figure 7-4. The competitive matrix.

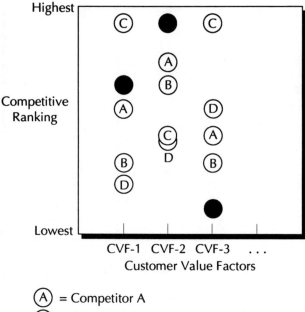

Note that some qualities or attributes may be much more highly valued by the customer than others. Ideally, of course, it would be best for your offering to surpass the competitors' in all aspects, but this is often not feasible. In most cases, it is important at least to get the highest scores on those attributes that most influence the customer's buying decisions.

It often happens that executives try to make these kinds of comparisons only to discover they don't have valid customer data to rely on. They often tend to resort to their own intuitive impressions, which could be dangerously distorted. This underscores the need for ongoing customer research, gathering information designed to serve just such a purpose.

All of these thinking models have as their purposes promoting clarity of thought, creating perspective, and getting consensus on the state of the enterprise in its environment. Before you can decide on the future you want to see exist, you must first know "what is." This kind of analysis can help, but the ultimate insights must come from somewhere deep in the gray matter of the leaders. There are subtle truths in every business, and simpleminded reactions from textbook wisdom can sometimes do more harm than good.

For example, the strictest interpretation of the "star and dog" theory of life cycles would suggest that a value package that is not showing a profit should be eliminated. However, its existence might have other catalytic benefits. It might represent a significant brand symbology, with a long history of customer recognition and awareness. If linked to other products, it can play a part in an overall portfolio concept even if it can't stand alone. Similarly, it might be a "loss leader" or a customer-access product, paving the way for continued business with those who buy it. You need to be sure you're not simply rationalizing away the avoidance of an unpleasant decision, but at the same time you need to connect the dots to create the picture of the total value proposition that you can take to the market.

Walls, Doors, and Windows: Customer Access

Throughout the discussion so far, we have frequently used the term *customer access*. This, in many ways, is one of the most critical concepts for the coming decades. Marketing is expensive. Large-scale advertising can devour resources at an alarming rate. These days, it takes a well-developed marketing infrastructure to get a product to the customer who might be willing to buy it. There are many entrepreneurs and inventors with wonderful ideas and valuable products to offer, but without customer access they will not succeed.

Customer access is becoming increasingly expensive and at the same time inefficient. The cost of reaching one customer with one selling message is rising all the time. And as mass markets disintegrate and microsegments appear, many of the traditional channels are not well enough focused. Firms are paying to communicate to people who are not really potential customers.

Probably the most horrifying example of this is the direct-mail industry, which includes catalog marketing firms in particular. A rented list of names may produce a response of 1 to 2 percent in orders. Typical direct-mail firms carry selling costs on the order of 30 to 40 percent of sales just to book their orders. With an additional 25 to 40 percent going to the cost of the goods they sell, and a significant chunk for labor, there is usually a tremendous squeeze on profit margins. This industry desperately needs new thinking about customer access.

Obviously, one of the first places to look for advantages is in *customer-base analysis.* This involves gathering data on the buying characteristics and profitability of the different varieties of customers in your portfolio, and ranking them in terms of real profit, that is, gross margin revenue compared to the cost of making the sale. If 5 to 10 percent of your customers account for two thirds of your real profit, does it make sense to invest the same amount to sell to every customer? Isn't it more productive to differentiate your customer-access strategies according to profitability and selling costs?

As another avenue for reducing the cost of customer access, a number of firms are launching actual customer-access products, that is, offerings that have the primary purpose of maintaining continuous contact with the customer base. The Volvo car company of Sweden encourages its dealers to sell auto insurance to their customers, not only because it is a natural "extension" product but also because it keeps the door open for continued selling. Volvo owners typically have long-term love affairs with their cars, and it often isn't difficult to sell them a replacement, but if you lose touch with them you have no way of knowing when they become candidates. And worse, you have to pay the customer-access costs all over again sometime in the future.

But the most obvious customer-access strategy of all is the one most widely neglected by a majority of businesses: *customer retention.* The old term *customer loyalty* has been around for so long that you'd think it was built into the very foundation of every business. Nothing could be farther from the truth. It's really quite amazing how many companies are willing to give away a huge slice of their revenue pie to win new customers in order to replace the ones they're driving away every day.

How many businesses do you know that actually make a determined policy of hanging on to their customers, *one by one?* How many customers find that they get progressively better treatment, care, and special attention the longer they've done business with a firm? Do the people in your bank know how long you've been doing business there? Do you get the same routine treatment when you need something done that the new customer gets? Every bank is in favor of customer retention, but very few are actually interested in doing anything to increase it.

As a frequent business traveler, I've often noticed this effect. I recently noticed the figures on a statement of frequent flier mileage I received from one of the largest airlines, showing that I was within a scant 20,000 miles of passing through one million miles with them. I thought, "Now here's an interesting test of a company's commitment to differentiating itself. When I go over a million miles, will anything special happen? Will they send me a special card or a letter or a pen-and-pencil set? Will the president of the airline come to my office and shake my hand?" It doesn't take psychic powers to guess the result. A million miles came and went: no fanfare.

I often stay in a certain hotel in the city of Honolulu, which I visit fairly often on business. In fact, I probably stay at this particular hotel about thirty to forty nights per year. And yet, each time I show up to check in, there is not the slightest glimmer of recognition on the part of the front desk staff, who always seem to be new faces. In the modern computer age, it would seem to be a fairly simple matter for the reservation system to cue the front-desk person that this particular guest is a long-term customer. The priorities are all directed elsewhere. Sure, we all want customer retention. It's just that most of us don't want to be bothered to do anything to achieve it.

Would you like an example of customer-consciousness? Here's one. Some time ago I was invited to sit in on an operations meeting of the chief executive and the department heads of the elegant Mandarin Oriental Hotel in Hong Kong. The forty-five-minute conference had only one item on the agenda: the individual guests who were leaving the hotel that day and the new ones who were coming in. As the marketing director read each name, each of the department heads offered any pertinent comments about that particular guest's stay, and they dealt with any matters that might affect the person's desire to return.

When the manager of the hotel read the first name on the new-arrival list, the marketing manager consulted his computer print-out and observed, "Mr. and Mrs. X are here for their thirty-fourth visit to the hotel. They would like a Rolls-Royce pickup at the airport, and they would like to have some fresh fruit in their room. They would like to take a nap as soon as they arrive, and they prefer not to be disturbed for a few hours." Right on down the list they went, person by person, not reservation by reservation. There was no discussion of occupancy rate, no talk of food costs, no treatment of maid-service hours used. There were only individual customers coming in and going out. Of course they have meetings to deal with all kinds of operational matters, and particularly operating costs, but at this meeting they were thinking about customers.

Harvard professor Earl Sasser has studied the economics of customer retention in some depth. He says:

> The concept of customer retention may be one of the secret weapons of the nineties, and a well-kept secret it is. Virtually every competent study I know about shows that an investment in customer retention repays itself with a greater multiplier than almost any profit-building option you can name, including brand advertising. The amazing thing is that so many companies invest heavily in marketing and yet do so little to retain the customers they have.[3]

Strategic Partnering: How to Leverage Resources

One of the hallmarks of the next decade of business will surely be an increase in *partnering* among organizations. As the post-capitalist model of the value-creating enterprise becomes ever more prevalent, even among smaller firms, it makes more and more sense to leverage resources rather than try to own resources. This is not to say that acquisitions and stock-sharing arrangements will disappear, or even become insignificant. But they may represent the less preferred way of doing things rather than the favorite way. And the Opportunity Scan for just about any enterprise should at least consider the possibilities offered.

Partnering can take a variety of forms. It already exists in many areas in the form of special distribution arrangements; licenses and rights to use intellectual property such as patents, trademarks, and copyrights; buying cooperatives; and various cooperative marketing activities. But it can also include jointly owned ventures that take advantage of the capabilities of each player. And it can extend to less formally defined arrangements and even network-style marketing methods.

Pick up almost any issue of *The Wall Street Journal,* London's *Financial Times,* or almost any financial newspaper in any major city, and you'll see reports of new alliances developing among key players in various industries.

One of the biggest alliances in recent years is the merger of cellular telephone marketer McCaw Communications into AT&T, in a $12 billion stock arrangement, to form a marketing powerhouse in the telecommunications industry. As continuing deregulation and technological forces such as digital electronics, fiber-optic signal transmission, cellular telephones, and image technology cause a fundamental restructuring of a number of industries, telephone companies, cellular-phone companies, cable-TV operators, and video programming companies are all whirling around the dance floor looking for partners that can help them get a bigger share of the business.

These various acquisitions, alliances, and partnerships will certainly accelerate the development of the technology as well as expand market demand by making attractive new products available more quickly than otherwise possible. This is also a worldwide phenomenon. British Telecom acquired a major share in MCI Communications, AT&T's fast-growing competitor. Other telecoms will certainly follow that lead in similar areas.

Partnering, if skillfully arranged, can offer a number of benefits to an enterprise, particularly a small-to-medium-size one that needs to grow its competitive base. These advantages can include:

- Increased customer access
- Enhanced market image and credibility thanks to favorable associations with successful players

- Access to valuable new technology
- Access to needed capital
- Shared risk in research and development investments
- Access to the basic entrepreneurial know-how in a particular industry
- Shared use of common infrastructure, such as manufacturing, distribution, or warehousing
- Circumventing political barriers by joining up with existing enterprises that have already situated themselves comfortably

However, not all alliances are made in heaven, and not all of them succeed. There are quite a few that fail to provide the synergy hoped for, and some that even turn into nightmares.

The Scandinavian Airlines System, for example, embarked on a very ambitious effort to create a "global travel company." Under the leadership of its visionary chairman, Jan Carlzon, who made a name in the early 1980s for masterminding the turnaround of SAS based on service management methods, the company sought to forge alliances with various kinds of travel companies around the world. The idea was to integrate air travel, hotel accommodation, car rental, recreation and tour services, local transportation, and a variety of related offerings into a seamless pathway of service to any one customer. In theory, the customer could travel from a home city to a city in a foreign land, do business, take time to vacation, and return home, all while in the care and custody of this network of providers.

It seemed like a great idea, but it turned out to be a bite too big to chew. The complexity of the alliances in the airline industry alone, together with a number of other distractions facing SAS, not the least of which was a financial hemorrhage resulting from its coventure with Houston-based Continental Airlines, conspired to bog the whole thing down. Although Carlzon's concept represented the quintessence of the post-capitalist model, it was simply too ambitious an undertaking at that time.

A similar sobering experience confronted Federal Express Corporation when it tried to move out of its very successful home market in North America and create a presence in Europe. With great confidence, the company set up operations in

Belgium and worked out handoff arrangements for parcels moving back and forth across the Atlantic. However, it quickly found that the established networks of business relationships were hard to crack. European customers didn't fall over their own feet seeking to do business with a newcomer.

And the naïve concept of "pan-European marketing" that had been pushed by a number of American experts turned sour as FedEx leaders had to face the fact that Europe is still a collection of parochial national business cultures, not a monolithic market. After about a year of very significant losses, FedEx abruptly withdrew from the Continental market, contenting itself to be a freight hauler of parcels across the Atlantic, allowing other established carriers to handle local distribution.

More recently, SAS has engaged in unsuccessful discussions with KLM Royal Dutch Airlines, Swissair, and Austrian Airlines to create a combined organization that could have become the largest international carrier in Europe. This is increasingly characteristic of situations in which companies that had been fierce competitors have cast their lots together, hoping to accomplish more by synergy than they could by competition.

If you believe the post-capitalist enterprise model has merit, it pays to consider carefully the kinds of alliances that might be feasible for your enterprise. Yours might not be one of the megacorporations reported about in the financial press, but alliance thinking can make sense for organizations of all sizes and in all kinds of business. It might be that a well-conceived alliance or network of alliances with other enterprises with synergistic interests could open new doors for all involved. Certainly any alliance strategy should be approached with great care and a dash of realism. But an element of creativity and boldness can also go a long way toward making it pay off.

Notes

1. "Down-to-Earth Ads Are Aimed at Those Thinking of Heaven," *Wall Street Journal*, August 13, 1993, p. 1.
2. Clem Sunter, *The World and South Africa in the 1990s* (Cape Town: Human & Rousseau, 1987), pp. 74–78.
3. Speech in Mexico City.

Chapter 8

Model Building 101: The Customer Value Model

It is a capital mistake to theorise in advance of the facts.

"Sherlock Holmes"

Beyond Product and Service: Think Customer Value

The arbitrary distinction implied by the two terms *product* and *service* may turn out to be one of the biggest historical thinking mistakes ever made by business leaders. The vocabulary of business is largely organized around the notion that some companies sell products while others sell services. Presumably, under this distinction, some sell both. And, supposedly, those that sell products are supposed to think about service, too.

Unfortunately, the definition of *service* has been distorted by conventional business thinking. Traditionally, service has been construed to mean some sort of person-to-person interaction that's supposed to make the customer happy after the sale of a product. Customer service, as it was traditionally defined, amounted to a necessary evil, a labor cost incurred if the customer was dissatisfied with the product and wanted to return it or have it made right. Some business writers still refer to service as an "envelope" of added value wrapped around a tangible product.

This kind of archaic thinking leaves out an enormous range of value-creating businesses that have no "product." Health care, for instance, which in most developed countries amounts to 10 percent or more of gross national product, is a service with no deliverable product at its core. So is entertainment. So is travel. So is the hospitality industry. In fact, well over half of the money spent in any first-world economy buys nothing tangible. And yet much of Western business thinking still clings to the obsolete mind-set that "real business" is all about making and selling products. Services, in this mind-set, are considered secondary and derivative.

Many economists are still trying to make outdated distinctions between so-called manufacturing industries and so-called service industries, with diminishing success. A thought-provoking article in *The Economist*, titled "The Final Frontier," shows why this is now a useless distinction:

> The growth of services is nothing new. As early as 1900 America and Britain both had more jobs in services than in industry. By 1950 services employed half of all American workers. Last year the figure hit 76%.
>
> Meanwhile, the share of manufacturing has fallen in all the big economies. It now accounts for only 23% of America's GDP (and an even smaller 18% of jobs). In Britain and Canada manufacturing has tumbled to less than 20% of total output. Even in Japan and Germany, manufacturing is now no more than 30% of GDP.
>
> Some economists argue that the boom in services is caused mainly by firms contracting out jobs they used to do for themselves, such as catering, advertising, and data processing. But studies in America and Britain suggest that this explains only a fraction of the increase.
>
> If anything, official figures may underestimate the true importance of services in both output and jobs, as many activities in manufacturing firms are really services.
>
> Government number-crunchers stick *The Econo-*

mist, along with all newspapers, in the manufacturing sector, even though few employees actually make anything. The work of a freelance journalist, by contrast, is counted in the service sector. *The division between services and manufacturing is becoming steadily less useful.* [Italics supplied.]

Take General Motors, the archetypal manufacturer. Its biggest single supplier is not a steel or glass firm, but a health care provider, Blue Cross–Blue Shield. In terms of output, one of GM's biggest "products" is financial and insurance services, which together with EDS, its computing-services arm, account for a fifth of total revenue.[1]

Some business leaders, business writers, and political people seem to have a romantic fixation with "manufacturing" as the true engine of society, the true job creator, and the only really legitimate economic dimension of a modern country. They lament the decline of the "industrial base" and call boldly for "reindustrialization." Yet manufacturing leveled off years ago, just as farming leveled off decades ago, in terms of the proportion of the population it occupies in creating value for the society.

As any national economy develops, a small fraction of the workforce can eventually produce enough food for everyone, and the rest become available for manufacturing, which begins to play its part in adding to the quality of life with an abundance of useful or enjoyable things. And as manufacturing levels off, the services sector that grows right along side it continues growing and eventually provides work for a larger and larger percentage of the people. This is a normal economic progression.

So the distinction between manufacturing and serving is now arbitrary and obsolete. In the modern sense, all work is service work. Why should bolting a bumper onto an automobile be thought of as any more fundamental or more special than delivering a parcel, cooking a meal, answering a telephone, programming a computer, or performing brain surgery? The skills and outcomes are different, but both have the fundamental purpose of meeting needs, solving problems, and adding value for human beings. Both require knowledge, tools, and technology. Both happen in specialized environments. And ultimately, both are services. Call it manufacturing if you like, but fabrication and assembly is simply one particular type of value-creating work. It is neither more nor less important, neither more nor less noble than any other.

The new lexicon of business goes beyond manufacturing industries and service industries. It goes beyond product and customer service, beyond hardware and software. The new defining precept is *customer value.*

What is customer value? It's the "mindware" created by the hardware and software you provide. It's the customer's perception of specific need fulfillment. It's the end condition that the customer considers worthy of his or her approval. This may seem a bit broad, but it enables us to think of customer value in comprehensive terms. This can cover everything from a tangible piece of merchandise to a pure experience. In either case, the value is not in the thing or experience we deliver; the value is in the result perceived by the customer.

For example, most people have gas and electricity in their homes. Most of them don't want gas or electricity; they want what the gas and electricity can do for them: create light, warmth, heat for cooking, music, entertainment, and so on. Why does a person buy a pet? Take an airplane trip? Buy vitamins? Go to a movie? Buy a VCR? Customer value is in the outcomes people seek, not the thing or experience they pay for.

Sometimes a physical, deliverable item is far more important in the customer's mind than anything accompanying it. Other times there is no deliverable, or the deliverable plays a very minor role. Regardless, it is the *total perception of value* on the part of the customer that counts.

After decades of defining customer value mostly in terms of merchandise characteristics, and largely going on intuition with regard to subjective results, we are having to learn how to discover the rules of value that exist in the customer's own mind. It is more and more dangerous to operate on intuition, guesswork, and assumptions in designing the *customer value package* we offer. We must use methods of inquiry to discover how the customer defines value in his or her own life and world. And we must be willing to take those truths seriously in developing the strategy of the business.

Finding the "Invisible Truth"

Historians report that the Greek philosopher Aristotle believed women had fewer teeth than men. The way he arrived at that conclusion was very simple: He just decided it must be so. And that's the same way many executives today come to believe what they believe about their customers.

After twenty years of working with organizations, I've reluctantly arrived at a fairly basic axiom:

> The longer you've been in business, the greater the probability you don't really understand what's going on in the minds of your customers.

There is a certain arrogance of tenure that blocks many organizational leaders from innocent-minded inquiry into their customers' attitudes.

Ignorance or misconceptions about the psyche of the customer can lead people down the wrong road in trying to implement "quality programs" in organizations, for example. Too many quality initiatives start by measuring and counting tangible work products and processes, without any evidence that improving them would contribute to the ultimate success of the business.

The "quality movement" in all major countries is headed inexorably in one direction: *customer focus.* Any quality-improvement effort that does not contribute to adding value for customers, either external or internal, is misdirected. And how can we create customer value in a way that's cost-effective and profitable if we don't know what the customer values?

Aristotle's faulty notions about women and their teeth— and probably other subjects—presumably influenced his behavior accordingly. Just like Aristotle, if we have distorted notions about what is motivating the customer's choices, we will behave inappropriately with respect to winning and keeping the customer's business.

Aristotle could have relieved his self-imposed ignorance by the simple act of asking Mrs. Aristotle to open her mouth so that he could count her teeth. Instead, he conjured up the "facts" in his own mind. This kind of "Aristotelian" thinking dominates a great deal of the design and delivery of customer value today. And it is reflected in a great number of strategic plans.

One of the largest insurance companies in North America invested heavily in a performance standard its executives considered paramount in importance: a five-day turnaround in issuing its policies. The time from when the selling agent placed the order until the document left the building had to be no more than five days, 90 percent of the time. The company invested heavily in the standard, preached it, measured it, and enforced it. However, when we conducted some very basic customer-value research for the firm, we never found a single person—agent or insured—who cared about getting the policy in five days. The performance standard created no value for the customers.

This is a very common occurrence. Hotels, restaurants, hospitals, cruise lines, and many other types of business throw "quality surveys" and questionnaires at their customers, basing their questions on Aristotelian criteria conjured up in the minds of the marketing people rather than developed by skillful customer research. Many other businesses don't ask for customer feedback at all, to say nothing of having valid models of customer value.

McDonald's Corporation found out that sometimes the only way to be sure about certain aspects of customer value is to actually offer something to the customer and see what happens. Its highly promoted "McLean" burger went into American stores with great fanfare about healthy new American lifestyles. The ultra–low-fat burger met with resounding apathy. After about two years of promotion, the McLean accounted for only about 2 percent of the burgers sold. In the early customer research, many Americans said they wanted a low-fat product, but when it came to putting their money down, most of them opted for the original high-fat Big Mac.

Mars, Inc., had a similar experience in testing a low-calorie chocolate bar, the Milky Way II, which used a Procter & Gamble food substance called caprenin to simulate the familiar "mouth feel" of high-fat milk chocolate. Hershey Foods also abandoned a low-calorie, low-fat chocolate bar when customer tests showed that people apparently didn't value healthy eating enough to switch from the familiar products. Product questions like those can often be very difficult to answer reliably in customer research.

Disney Corporation had to make a very heavy capital commitment before discovering that the French don't necessarily respond to Mickey Mouse and friends the same way Americans and people from many other countries do. The Euro Disney park outside of Paris achieved surprisingly little support from French customers and could not attract enough other Europeans to make it profitable. Facing losses of over $300 million in its first two years, Disney management had to rethink the entire venture.

In *The Only Thing That Matters: Bringing the Power of the Customer Into the Center of Your Business*, I referred to having special insights into the customer's thinking as the ability to perceive the "invisible truth."[2] You can look at market statistics all day without seeing it. You can run demographic studies and shred the data in fifty directions without discovering it. The way you find the invisible truth is to listen directly to your customers as they talk about their worlds, their problems, their needs, and their interests. The more innocent and open-minded you can be about hearing what they say, the greater the chance you'll discover one or more elements of their experience that present a special opportunity for your enterprise to create superior value. This is the real objective of customer research, finding that invisible truth.

The discussion in *The Only Thing That Matters* offered the analogy of the eye test many of us took when we were young. The school nurse showed us a card with lots of colored dots all grouped into a tight circle. All the dots were the same color except for a pattern of dots in the middle which, in a different color, formed a familiar symbol such as the number 8. The task was to recognize the embedded 8. People who could see the number had normal color vision; those who could not had some degree of perceptual deficiency.[3] To use that analogy, finding the invisible truth is like perceiving the embedded number. You have to approach the truth with the right perceptual mind-set, and when you see it, it becomes obvious and compelling.

If we're going to make our strategy-development approach customer-focused, we must find the invisible truth—the customer's perception of value. By using the methods of customer-perception research, we can identify the *customer value model*, or CVM, a set of critical criteria that constitute the customer's perception of value in the entire experience of doing business with us. To do that, let's take a closer look at the psychology behind customer value.

The Hierarchy of Customer Value

It makes good sense to think of customer value as forming a hierarchy analogous to Abraham Maslow's famous hierarchy of needs. This *hierarchy of customer value* has four levels, from lowest to highest:

1. *Basic*—the fundamental components of your customer value package required just to be in business. If you're a retail establishment, for example, you must have a location that's clean, properly furnished and fixtured, properly staffed, and properly stocked.

2. *Expected*—what your customers consider "normal" for you and your competitors. If you're an airline company, they expect you to have competitive prices, convenient schedules, edible food, and reasonably civil customer-contact employees.

3. *Desired*—added-value features that the customers know about and would like to have but don't necessarily expect because of the current level of performance of your competitors. This is the first level of possible differentiation and superiority over your competitors. If you're a hospital, it means *consistently* friendly and caring staff, accurate and honest information about the patient's condition, systems and procedures that engender trust and confidence, and cooperative interactions with the patient's family members and significant others.

4. *Unanticipated*—added-value features that go well beyond the learned expectations and desires the customer brings to the experience of doing business with you. It may be unusually fast turnaround, an unusually confidence-inspiring guarantee, unusual expertise on the part of your employees, advanced merchandise features, or many other possibilities. These are "surprise" features that can set you apart from your competitors and win you the loyalty of customers—*if*, of course, they really do add significant value in the eyes of your customers.

Figure 8-1 illustrates this hierarchy of customer value as a stair-step progression.

Note that you must have mastered the first two levels of the customer value hierarchy just to compete on an equal footing. This does not make your offering particularly attractive in the customer's mind. You must get beyond "customer satisfaction" and move to the Desired or Unanticipated levels of value in order to make a difference.

Bear in mind, however, that features at the Desired and Unanticipated levels do little good if other features at the Basic and Expected levels are poorly done. A hospital that offers all private rooms, gourmet food, and personal luxuries to its patients won't get far if the place is dirty, the staff is cold and indifferent, and the meals are late. The hierarchy of customer

Figure 8-1.   The hierarchy of customer value.

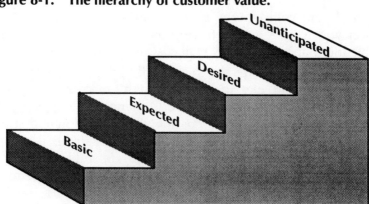

value is progressive and cumulative: Each level builds upon the levels below it.

Companies that offer superior customer value are those whose leaders have freed themselves from Aristotelian thinking, who have learned what their customers really value, and who constantly push their organizations to achieve that value.

Building the Customer Value Model

Suppose you are relocating to another city and need to have your household belongings moved. You call a moving and storage firm to get some information. As you start planning the move, you get to thinking about experiences you've had with movers in the past. In deciding whether this particular moving firm will be acceptable, you inevitably start thinking about a few critical quality factors that are important to you in having your personal belongings moved. How will they handle the delicate items? Can you trust the employees not to steal anything? Will the price be reasonable? Will they be agreeable and easy to work with, or will you get two Neanderthal characters who just throw your stuff into the truck?

All of these factors going through your mind are part of your *customer value model*. It stands to reason, doesn't it, that the company whose salespeople show you that they understand your customer value model better than their competitors are in a better position to win your business. Well, it works the same way for any business, including yours. If you have an accurate fix on how your customers are defining value—from their own selfish points of view, not yours—you can capitalize on that information to make sure your organization delivers that value exceedingly well.

Defined more precisely, a customer value model is:

> A set of critical indicators used by the customer to evaluate the quality of the outcomes you provide.

Customer value models can be fairly simple, but that doesn't mean they are always easy to build. There are at least two difficulties that arise in the way most enterprises approach customer value:

1. *Relying on intuition*. Most organizations do not use an explicit set of critical indicators; instead, they tend to rely on vague, unstated, intuitively held beliefs about "what the customer wants." This makes it almost impossible to communicate a common message throughout the organization, and to focus people's attention on the critical factors that win and keep the customer's business.

2. *Aristotelian thinking*. Many organizations that do use explicit customer value criteria don't exercise the discipline of deriving the criteria from the minds of their customers and validating them in solid customer research. Believing they know what's important to their customers, they simply conjure up a list of factors and never verify their guesswork.

Customer value models can change over time. When British Airways launched a major customer-research project in the early 1980s, they asked fliers how important they felt it was for the airplane to leave on time. Shortly before that, Scandinavian Airlines had made a major marketing advantage out of on-time takeoff, achieving the position of being the most punctual airline in Europe. But a few short years later, the customers were saying "What do you mean, take off on time? We *expect* you to take off on time. Do you think you deserve extra credit just for doing what you're supposed to do?" On-time takeoff had moved downward on the hierarchy of customer value from a desired feature to an expected feature. Customer thinking had been reconditioned by the rising competitive performance in the industry, triggered by SAS's first breakthrough.

There is a new factor that may eventually emerge in the CVMs of airline customers, after one or more airline companies do something about it. That factor is the onboard air quality. Many people get off airplanes after flights of three hours or more feeling groggy, tired, and vaguely uncomfortable. The catchphrase *jet lag* may not accurately describe what they're feeling. New studies are revealing that the stale air on long flights may be making flight attendants and passengers ill, because of the increased concentrations of airborne germs, dust, and carbon dioxide. Some frequent fliers have even taken to wearing surgical face masks to filter the air.

Some newer aircraft designs have actually reduced the amount of outside make-up air used to refresh the internal air supply, as a way of reducing the energy costs of processing the air. It is routinely taken for granted that onboard air is abnormally dry as well. This can dry out the delicate membranes in the nasal passages, cause tiny cracks in the tissue, and make people more susceptible to infections and nosebleeds.

Why does the air on a $30 million airplane have to be dry? And why should the customer have to sit at the pressurized equivalent of 5,000-foot altitude breathing rarefied air for many hours? Have you noticed how many people on an airplane fall asleep within a few minutes after the wheels leave the ground? Is it because they're tired, or because they're groggy from insufficient oxygen? Could the way they feel when they get off the plane be a version of altitude sickness, aggravated by breathing bad air? Might the onboard environment conspire to make the passengers groggy and therefore more docile, compliant, and easier to manage?

This could become one of the important differentiating elements of customer value in an industry where customers perceive very little difference between suppliers.

Hospitals have an interesting customer value proposition. Research into the perceptions of patients in hospitals clearly shows two value factors to be critical in the patient's willingness to return to a particular hospital and to recommend it highly to the physician, friends, and family. Yet, probably fewer than 20 percent of hospitals regularly measure these perceptions or do anything with the findings.

The first key factor is being helped to feel like an *empowered customer*. People in hospitals dislike feeling helpless, powerless, and treated like children who have no authority. Actions by hospital employees like briefing the customer on his or her condition, encouraging and answering questions, offering decisions and choices, and including the customer in decisions about treatment have been clearly shown to reinforce this customer feeling. Yet very few hospitals explicitly manage this factor.

The second key factor is *trust through perceived teamwork and continuity*. When the nurse gives the patient one piece of information or advice about his or her treatment and the doctor later walks in and gives information that is completely contradictory, the patient begins to have a trust problem. When a nurse comes in with the wrong medication or mistakes one patient for another, doubts begin to arise in the customer's mind. Incidents like these are very common with hospitals, and many hospital executives have no idea how frequently they're going on.

When I recently had eye surgery, I was asked by the surgical nurse just before being wheeled into the operating room, "Now, which eye is it?" There may have been a good reason behind that question, but it didn't make me feel very confident. The complex nature of hospital organizations virtually guarantees opportunities for things to go wrong, for people to miscommunicate, and for the ball to be dropped or lost between departments. The customer's perception of trust, teamwork, and continuity doesn't come by accident. It must be earned and managed, and few hospitals do it well.

It's remarkable how many executives discover, through open-minded and creative customer research, that their most firmly held beliefs about their customers' thinking processes are off the mark. One of the most strategically effective things the leaders of any enterprise can do is to set aside their established beliefs about customer value and take the question directly to the customers. By listening in an open-minded, innocent way, it is possible to discover the invisible truth that can make an enormous strategic difference if your competitors don't know it.

Of course, it's not enough just to know the secret invisible truth; you also have to implement that truth in the way your organization operates. That is the real challenge of the model-building process described in the following chapters.

Notes

1. "The Final Frontier," *The Economist*, February 1993.
2. Karl Albrecht, *The Only Thing That Matters: Bringing the Power of the Customer Into the Center of Your Business* (New York: HarperBusiness, 1992), p. 106.
3. Ibid.

Chapter 9

Model Building 102:
Vision, Mission, and Values

To make a great dream come true,
You must first have a great dream.

Hans Selye

Curing the "Mission Statement Blues"

Creating a meaningful vision statement or mission statement
for an enterprise seems to be one of the most frustrating and
least satisfying tasks executives have to face. And judging by
the dearth of really effective ones, we have to conclude most
don't face it very well. Countless executives and leadership
teams have wrestled with the task and have come away confused, disappointed, or exasperated. Others may think they've
accomplished it, but the fruits of their labors are singularly
ineffectual and unimpressive. Their vision and mission statements tend to be either vague, fluffy platitudes, or simplistic
statements of the obvious. Relatively few succeed in crafting a
statement that has meaning and power. There are mission
statements, and then there are mission statements.

Some executives have had such unsatisfying experiences

with vision and mission statements that they don't want to tangle with the problem again. Very often during a strategy formulation process, when the time comes for drafting or redrafting them all kinds of avoidance behavior arises. "We already have a mission statement; we don't need to go through that again," they'll say. Or, "Our mission statement isn't perfect, but let's not waste time tinkering with it." In the extreme case, one or more executives might grumble, "This mission statement business is a big waste of time. We always get into big debates and split hairs about the meaning of each word, or whose magic words are the best. Let's just get on with our business."

These feelings are quite understandable. Executives see themselves as skilled thinkers, and the thinking process involved in crafting a vision statement or a mission statement is difficult and frustrating. It is one of the most challenging intellectual processes leaders ever have to face, and many come up dry. They don't enjoy being frustrated, or feeling as if they don't know how to solve the puzzle. So they just declare it "no problem" and keep on moving. They've got the "mission statement blues."

But it's a mistake to just push on without a clear statement of vision and mission. If the leaders can't come to consensus among themselves on a statement that expresses the meaning of their enterprise—their northbound train—then what can they hope to say to the rest of the people in the organization that will make any sense to them? If all they have is platitudes, then they have no message at all. They might just as well put up signs all over the organization that say "Work Hard," "Do a Good Job," "We're a Team," and the timeless "The Customer Is King." In many ways, the vision or mission statement is a test of whether there really is a message. For the sake of discussion here, we'll simply use the term *mission statement* to refer to both the vision statement and the mission statement interchangeably, or to a combination of both in one statement if that's what you prefer.

There is a cure for the mission statement blues. It is a very simple trick. It doesn't guarantee you a powerful mission statement, but it will eliminate the major mistake that executive teams make in trying to draft mission statements. Here it is:

Separate the thinking from the "wordsmithing."

The most common cause of the frustrating wrangles that executives get into is confusing the journalism with the thinking. When they start out trying to draft a mission statement directly, they are almost sure to get into debates about the best choice of words. The better way is to work out the *basic idea* of the mission statement first, and then have somebody put some compelling words around that idea.

You're not ready to start drafting the language of your vision or mission statement until you have settled on a driving idea, the organizing principle behind the way you want to do business, and until you can write that idea down on the back of a business card. Once you have consensus on the core concept of your business, writing it out becomes a much more manageable process. I've often witnessed a sudden rise in energy and enthusiasm among an executive team at the point when they break through to the critical premise of the enterprise. After that, they're much more willing to push on with the process of getting the language right.

The Vision: What Do We Aspire to Be?

Many executives prefer to combine the vision statement and mission statement into a single statement rather than have two separate ones. Others go further and add a statement of philosophy and values. Still others add business goals or priorities. However, it seems that, at some point, it is worth breaking the message up into digestible, bite-size parts, even though they may all go into an overall document that becomes the total corporate credo, constitution, or whatever one may choose to call it. This is what I referred to in Chapter 4 as the strategic success model, or simply the strategic model, and I prefer to break it down into separate components. Although not everyone prefers that approach, I believe it works well. The remainder of the discussion here deals with separate statements of vision, mission, core values, and the related components described in the strategic success model given in Chapter 4.

What is a vision statement? Why, it is a statement of a *vision,* your vision for the enterprise. Literally, a vision for an organization is:

> An image of what the people of the enterprise aspire for it to be or become.

Note that the key word is *image.* It must be something that you can describe and that people can see in their mind's eye. It is a mental picture of the enterprise, operating in an environment, performing to some criterion of excellence, and appreciated for what it contributes.

What Makes an Effective Vision Statement?

Three components help to make a vision statement valid and useful for people:

1. *A focused concept*—something beyond platitudes; a value creation premise that people can actually picture as existing
2. *A sense of noble purpose*—something that is really worth doing; something that can create value, make a contribution, make the world a better place in some way, and win people's commitment
3. *A plausible chance of success*—something people can realistically believe to be possible and, if not perfectly attainable, at least plausible to strive for

Probably the easiest way to show how these three components go together to define your vision is to evaluate some examples. Playing the unenviable role of the professor, I'll offer a grade of A, B, C, D, or F on each of several real statements of real companies. Probably nobody else would agree with me completely, but the purpose of these examples is simply to illuminate the value of the three critical components just mentioned. These vision statements may not necessarily be the absolute latest versions, because many companies periodically revise their statements.

**Sabre Operations
(Computerized Reservation System of
American Airlines)**

To satisfy each external and internal customer by providing caring yet professional service that exceeds all our customers' expectations.

Grade: D

Comments: A generic, all-purpose statement that could apply to any business at all; it conveys a noble purpose, but we don't know whether it's for a construction company, a chain of funeral parlors, a government agency, or an information system.

British Royal Mail

As Royal Mail our mission* is to be recognised as the best organisation in the World delivering text and packages.

Grade: B+

Comments: Simple and easy to grasp. However, when a vision statement talks about being the best in the world, one has to ask whether it is credible, since there can be only one best. This is not to say it isn't a worthwhile statement; however, its framers have to be prepared to back it up. It will lose credibility if the people in the enterprise don't see their leaders taking it seriously.

---

*Although the wallet card calls it a mission, this is actually more of a vision statement.

**Department of Administrative Services
(Commonwealth of Australia)**

To be recognised by our customers and the government as Australia's best provider of services and a leader in public sector reform.

Grade: A

Comments: The grade I give to this vision statement cannot possibly be objective for two reasons: (1) I helped write it, and (2) interpreting it requires knowing that DAS is a government department that has set out to operate with commercial practices. It provides services to other government departments, but it does so on a direct-charge, for-profit basis, and it competes with private-sector service providers in most of its categories. This accounts for the part of the statement dealing with being a leader in public-sector reform. DAS executives believe that all government organizations, in all countries, should be moving toward this kind of model.

The Mission: How Should We Do Business?

In contrast to the vision statement, which presents an image of what we aspire to be or become, the mission statement tells how we are going to do business in order to fulfill the vision. The vision is the place we want to go to or the journey we want to take; the mission is the means for traveling. In order to achieve the state of affairs projected by the vision, the enterprise must *create value* in its chosen way, thereby succeeding in its environment.

What Makes an Effective Mission Statement?

Although not all authors may agree exactly on the best form for an effective mission statement, I believe it should define at least the following three things:

1. *The customer*—defined not in terms of some market segment or statistical category, but in terms of a basic defining *need premise* that leads that person (or entity) to consider doing business with your enterprise
2. *The value premise*—defined not in terms of what your organization does, makes, sells, or delivers, but in terms of the fundamental *value* it represents in matching the customer's need premise
3. *What makes you special*—your special *means for creating value*, in order to win and keep the customer's business

Probably the easiest way to show how the three components of customer-need premise, delivered-value premise, and means for creating value go together to define your mission is to evaluate some examples. Again playing the proverbial professor, I'll offer a grade of A, B, C, D, or F on each of a number of real statements of real companies. Again, the purpose of these examples is simply to illuminate the value of the three critical components mentioned. As with the vision statements, these particular mission statements may not necessarily be the absolute latest versions.

Levi Strauss & Co.

The mission of Levi Strauss & Co. is to sustain profitable and responsible commercial success by marketing jeans and selected casual apparel under the Levi's brand.

Grade: C

Comments: Doesn't dramatize a customer need premise; doesn't convey the value premise of the product; gives no clue about how the company sustains the hundred-year love affair it has had with its customers. The statement doesn't even mention the word *customer* or refer to any particular identifying characteristic of the buyer of the product. All it really says is, "We sell clothes with the Levi's brand label." In the 500-word statement that goes with this lead statement, the term *customer* appears only once, in the very last paragraph.

Many corporate mission statements emphasize "profit," "profitable growth," or "commercial success." Others may disagree, but I believe statements about being profitable or commercially successful are basic to the assumptions of the business and do not belong in the mission statement. Being commercially successful is, for most firms, a defining purpose of their existence, not a mission. In my definition, the mission statement tells how you are going to do business, not merely that you are in business.

Hilton Hotel Corporation

To be recognized as the world's best first-class, commercial hotel organization, to constantly strive to improve, allowing us to prosper as a business for the benefit of our shareholders, our guests, and our employees.

Grade: B –

Comments: Mostly platitudes; nothing unique or compelling about the message; written mostly in financial language, not human language. It does position the enterprise as operating first-class hotels, although the term *commercial* seems obscure in this statement. But again, if you take out the stuff about profit, all it says is, "We operate first-class hotels."

Hershey Foods Corporation

Hershey Foods Corporation's Mission is to become a major diversified food company and a leading company in every aspect of our business as:

- The number one confectionery company in North America, moving toward worldwide confectionery market share leadership.
- A respected and valued supplier of high quality, branded, consumer food products in North America and selected international markets.

Grade: C

Comments: Wall Street language; the statement is informative, but it has no "heart." It's all about products, market share, and market leadership, which are admirable from the executive frame of reference. I doubt it would turn on very many employees.

Cathay Pacific Airlines
Our Service Commitment
The Mission

To achieve consistent upward growth in the total quality of inflight service and in the support we give to each other.

Grade: B+

Comments: Strong focus on the customer value premise, that is, service quality, and on the teamwork involved. However, it seems a bit telegraphic, or truncated, as if some final-draft version was brutally chopped down by the person who had the last word. It focuses on only the inflight experience; it needs to be widened to encompass the whole customer value premise, unless it is one of several related statements that do the whole job. On the back of the wallet card that has this statement, there are six "mission goals," which supply very well-phrased criteria for evaluating the way the cabin crew fulfill the mission.

Kowloon-Canton Railway (based in Hong Kong)

Our mission is to provide quality transport and related services in Hong Kong and with China in a safe, reliable, caring, cost-effective and environmentally responsible manner.

Grade: B+ to A−

Comments: Terse but fairly complete; doesn't focus strongly on the customer value premise, but does emphasize key criteria such as being safe, reliable, caring, etc.

Rodale Press (publisher of health and self-help books)

Our mission is to show people how they can use the power of their bodies and minds to make their lives better. "You can do it," we say on every page of our magazines and books.

Grade: A

Comments: Puts the customer value premise right up front; tells how they do it, and what business they're in. As we'll see later, this statement has the extra advantage of being very brief and memorable, without being bland and meaningless. This is a statement that both customers and employees can relate to, which is unusual for most mission statements.

"Po' Folks" Restaurants (country style cooking)

We always want to be the friendliest place you'll ever find to bring your family for great tasting, homestyle cooking, served with care and pride in a pleasant country-home setting at reasonable prices.

Grade: A+

Comments: This tells just about everything. It's also an example of a message that can be both a statement for the people of the company and an appeal to their customers. It has a clear customer-need premise, a clear value-delivery premise, and a sense of specialness, that is, a pleasant country-home setting. If you were a manager or an employee of a Po' Folks restaurant, wouldn't this mission give you a lot to go on, presuming it is supported with other information about implementing it operationally?

As previously emphasized, a mission statement doesn't

have to follow any particular format or contain any particular magic words. But the words need to carry a strong underlying message. It should say more than "We sell such-and-such a product," or "We operate in such-and-such markets," or "We will be the best doer of such-and-such in the world." Anybody can simply write down the organization's activity statement. But it takes a bit of insight to work backward from what you do to find the essential premise that makes you different from others.

To summarize the criteria, an effective mission statement should be:

1. *Definitive.* It defines the customer and his or her need premise, the value-delivery premise to be offered, and the means for putting the two together; it tells the story of our way of doing business.
2. *Identifying.* It makes clear which enterprise it refers to or at least narrows it down to a well-defined kind of enterprise; interchangeable platitudes won't do.
3. *Concise.* It makes the point in about one fairly simple paragraph; the only exception might be a statement that combines a sense of vision, mission, and values into one, in which case it might well be somewhat longer. But a basic mission statement should be something you can easily write on the back of a business card.
4. *Actionable.* It gives a person reading it some idea of what it looks like in operation, and what kinds of actions are involved in delivering on it.
5. *Memorable.* A good case in point is JFK's goal of "landing a man on the moon" ". . . before this decade is out."

After you draft the mission statement, it makes sense to evaluate it carefully using these five criteria. After the executives decide it sounds great, take it to a sample of ordinary humans, including middle managers, unit leaders, and working people. Ask them to evaluate it against the five criteria, and ask them to explain what kind of an organization might have and live by such a mission statement. If it makes good sense to them, and it says something worth saying, you've probably got it.

Our Core Values: What Do We Stand For?

John Foster, chief executive of NovaCare, stepped up on the speaker's platform to address the 400 key managers in the company. They were assembled to review the firm's business picture, and to go to work on the issues they had identified in connection with making their strategic plan come true.

"Our values," he said, "are the driving force behind the way we do business. We are a clinical organization. Our primary competitive resource is the therapist, the clinician, the specialist. These are the people who create the results that pay our salaries. While all of us have a contribution to make, we must all keep our minds on the basic core values of our enterprise.

"Our credo," Foster continued, "is 'Helping Make Life a Little Better.' Our four most basic beliefs are respect for the individual, service to the customer, pursuit of excellence, and commitment to personal integrity. Our credo, purpose, and beliefs must guide everything we do."

The two-day strategy conference, including the presentation to the managers that Foster had asked me to make, focused on the proposition of translating these values into business success.

Surely there are more than four values that are important to NovaCare's business. There are all kinds of values about honesty, fair business dealing, equal opportunity, patriotism, and many others. But Foster and his leadership team wanted to focus on these particular *core values*. Core values are the critical few that must guide the day-to-day behavior of everyone in the organization, if it is to be successful in achieving its mission.

Core values that would make sense for Volvo Corporation would likely not be the same ones for Qantas Airlines. Values for National Westminster Bank in England would probably not be right for Beth Israel Hospital in Boston. Union Bank of

Finland and Sony Corporation are two vastly different businesses, based in different national cultures and doing business in very different ways. Each needs its own unique set of core values.

The process of choosing core values may be quite simple, but the thinking process involved is not necessarily simple. One of the first questions the leaders of an enterprise need to ask themselves is, "What seem to be the actual core values of the organization right now?" Are there unconsciously held "phantom" values that are more powerful than any that might currently appear on a formal list in the chief executive's office? What are the real values we are subjecting people to?

Do the values say that, to get ahead around here you have to walk, talk, think, and act like the chief executive? Or is it acceptable to disagree with the boss? Do the values say that everybody has an equal shot at a high-ranking job, except for women? Do they say that any idea is welcome, unless it comes from somebody unimportant or unless it contradicts the basic beliefs of the leaders? Do the real values say that it's OK to mislead, deceive, or actually lie to customers rather than inconvenience ourselves?

An important part of the organizational scan, as previously mentioned, is a brutally honest appraisal of the actual values that are at work in the organization. If we don't like what we find out, we have to start thinking carefully about how those got to be the real core values, and what we have to do to substitute a new set of values.

This is an area where executive hypocrisy can be severely tested. One organization I worked with had appointed a special working group to develop a new statement of values. They had some great ideas on the list, such as "open and honest communication" and "tolerance for controversy," but it quickly became apparent that they were very different from the way the organization actually operated. They all knew that this new list of values would meet with snickers of cynicism throughout the organization, and so the statement of values got tabled indefinitely.

It is a useful process during the development of the strategic success model to perform a gap analysis on the core values. This involves forming a list of the real values that seem to be operating, and comparing them with the new list of core values that will be instrumental in carrying out the mission and achieving the vision. Any gap between the two presents the leaders with a problem in credibility. They must somehow help the people in the organization evolve a new set of "real" values and start living by them.

Beyond the Platitudes

There is no one, standard list of core values. The process of selecting a few key precepts as the basis of the value system deserves a great deal of thought on the part of the leaders of the enterprise. Unfortunately, many executive teams settle for a few worthy platitudes rather than think through carefully what they really need to emphasize. They may miss a very valuable opportunity to lend focus and meaning to what people do. When an enterprise has a strong set of values and its leaders stand up for those values in everything they do, the people in the organization perceive it as having a heart, a real and meaningful culture. When it has a list of homilies nobody really takes seriously, clearly the executives are in the habit of saying things they don't really mean.

This is not to say that there are any positive values that are actually unimportant in the business, only that people can't focus on fifty different values with the same degree of intensity. Certainly it's important to be honest. It's important to have equal opportunities for everyone to get ahead. It's important that people see the rewards from their contributions. Of course product quality is important. Of course customer satisfaction is important. They are all important, and so are dozens of other values. But which ones are super-important? Which ones convey the essence of the northbound train?

Nordstrom Corporation, the highly respected Seattle-based retailer of upscale clothing and related goods, has a very simple way of communicating the company values to its employees. They don't call it a formal statement of values. In fact, it's the basic employee handbook, but it only has one page. It says:

**WELCOME TO
NORDSTROM**

We're glad to have you with
our Company.
Our number one goal is to provide
outstanding customer service.
Set both your personal and
professional goals high.
We have great confidence in your
ability to meet them.
Nordstrom Rules:
Rule #1: *Use your good
judgment in all situations.*
There will be no additional rules.
Please feel free to ask
your department manager,
store manager, or division general
manager any question
at any time.
—nordstrom—

This is an important statement about core values: responsibility, freedom of action, respect for the individual, the obligations of leadership to serve those who serve.

The employees and managers of the Ritz-Carlton hotels evolved a statement of their philosophy—or values, if you prefer. It says:

We are ladies and gentlemen,
serving ladies and gentlemen.
We are always on stage.
Uncompromising levels of cleanliness
are the responsibility of everyone.
Be an ambassador for your hotel,
both inside and outside the workplace.

Whether you would have chosen this particular value message, or this particular format for expressing it, you'll probably agree that it is not a platitude. It has meaning and depth. It has heart. It speaks to people on a very human and personal level. And it is an important message that Ritz-Carlton people all know about and think about.

Forming the Corporate Credo

When the executives of the Department of Administrative Services, a part of Australia's Commonwealth government, got together in an intensive retreat to redefine the future of the organization, they succeeded in evolving a strategic concept for transforming their government department into a quasi-commercial enterprise, operating along the lines of a corporate entity. It was to remain a department of state, and yet it would sell its services at market prices to its many government customers. Even more challengingly, the government had decreed that virtually all of its customers would eventually be set free to acquire the same services from DAS's commercial competitors if they so chose.

DAS's executives knew that they would have to take the organization through a strategic and cultural transformation unlike anything ever done in the Australian government, and possibly in the world. After we had helped them develop the overall northbound train concept for the enterprise, the chief executive, Secretary Noel Tanzer, told them, "We've got to make sure every person in DAS understands what we're asking them to do, and what their part in it will be. We must put a solid set of values behind this transformation, and we must start living by them—right now."

During a very lively discussion, they proceeded to laundry-list a wide range of potential values, knowing they would eventually settle on a crucial few. As they kept referring to the vision, mission, customer value model, customer value package, and the results of the organizational scan, they were able to sort the many choices into primary and secondary categories. In the end, they selected a key set of values based on commercial thinking, strong leadership, and support to the employees who would be going through a very traumatic readjustment in their work lives.

There are more ways than one to engineer the actual process of formulating the credo for the enterprise. In Nova-Care's case, John Foster personally wrote the credo, purpose, and beliefs in consultation with his executives. In the case of DAS, Noel Tanzer and his leaders met with many of the group's managers and employees to test the overall strategic success model for validity, credibility, and focus. In other cases, executives may use an extensive process of employee meetings to get input, surface issues and concerns, and raise awareness of the need for a new direction. Ultimately, it is up to the leaders to formulate the direction, but there are various worthwhile methods for helping the people of the organization get connected to it.

More important than the form, format, or process for creating a valid and powerful corporate credo is actually *having* and using it as a leadership resource. Some people prefer to combine the vision, mission, and core values into a single document. Others like a simple statement which they prefer to call a vision statement. Others call it a mission statement. Some call it a statement of philosophy. Others simply call it "the way we do things." It really doesn't matter whether your definition of the northbound train follows the structure of the strategic success model presented in this book. It only matters that you have answered the critical questions of your business and expressed the answers in a form that people can understand, accept, and put to use in their work lives.

Chapter 10

Model Building 103:
Business Logic and Strategy

> There is one thing more powerful than all the armies
> of the world; and that is an idea whose time has
> come.
>
> Victor Hugo

What Is Your Business Logic?

Swedish management consultant Richard Normann is fond of
talking about the *business logic* of the enterprise. According to
Normann, "Every business has some kind of logic that organ-
izes its approach to things, whether that logic is conscious or
unconscious. It is surprising, however, how many organizations have a self-contradictory logic, or one that is inappropriate to what they're trying to become. It's important for the
leaders of any enterprise to consciously surface their business
logic and see whether it really makes sense."

Using Figure 10-1, let's develop this idea of business logic
and see how we might model it so that the leaders of the
organization can sort it out and make sure it works. We can
divide the overall logic of the business into four broad categories, or sublogics:

Figure 10-1. Business logic.

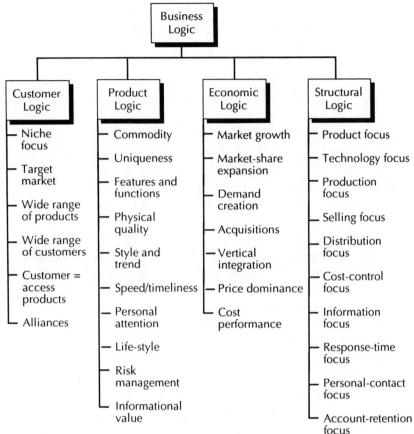

1. *The customer logic.* How shall we gain access to our customers?
2. *The product logic.* What value premise shall we take into the market? (The term *product*, in this discussion, refers very broadly to both physical merchandise and services provided, that is, the customer value.)
3. *The economic logic.* How are we going to get profit and growth, or achieve whatever criteria we set for economic performance?
4. *The structural logic.* How shall we organize ourselves to make the other three logics work together?

Let's review each of these four components of business logic in turn. Think about your own organization and about other organizations you know, and see how you might classify their business logic.

Your Customer Logic

There are a few basic ways to develop *customer access*, which is what marketing basically requires. The avenue or combination of avenues you choose must make sense for your line of business and the potential customers that might be interested. Here are some of the main choices for customer logic:

1. *Niche focus*—a narrowly defined value package that people buy under specific circumstances, such as car burglar alarms, vegetarian fast food, vacation tours to Norway, shiatsu massage, or real estate management software. You get the benefits of concentrated marketing by giving up options for a broader customer base. You must get customer access by being noticed or known when those customers perceive a specific need for what you offer.

2. *Target customer base*—a narrowly defined customer population, differentiated by some particular characteristic, such as retired people, golfers, teenagers, disabled people, psychiatric nurses, or stamp collectors. You can minimize the costs of market access by reaching these people through certain well-established channels, not having to pay for mass-market communications.

3. *Wide product range*—a range of things or value packages that enables you to do more business with selected customers by meeting a variety of needs; this includes variety stores and department stores, full-range insurance companies, full-service consulting firms, and companies that do turnkey development and construction. The wide range can focus on the needs of one target market or on a general consumer market.

4. *Wide customer range*—a true mass market approach, offering products or services that virtually anybody can buy, such as commodity foods, snacks and fast foods, haircuts,

gasoline, or banking services. Customer access usually involves being where the customers tend to be and differentiating yourself somehow from many competitors.

5. *Customer-access products*—a way of doing business that keeps you in contact with the customer so you can make future sales without having to pay the costs of customer access again. Also called continuity products, these include contracts for services, after-sale insurance, equipment maintenance plans, leasing instead of selling, subscriber products such as newsletters, and "until-forbid" programs such as a vitamin-of-the-month plan.

6. *Alliances*—teaming up with other suppliers to your intended customers, so you get increased customer access working with them. Physicians do this with referral networks, graphic artists do it by working with printing firms, photographers do it by working with graphic designers, and specialized consulting firms team up to handle large client projects. Alliances work best when the players have separate and distinct areas of interest that do not compete with one another, and when each lacks something the other can provide.

Probably no one company will find all of these avenues equally appealing. The logic of the business will usually favor one more than others. The value of thinking in these terms is in making the best use of the most promising channel for customer access.

Your Product Logic

There are many different types of focus you can apply in thinking about your product, meaning the customer-value premise you take into the marketplace. However, it helps to have some simple way to categorize the product in terms of customer appeal. Your product logic answers the question, What is the essential, differentiating value premise built into this offering? Some of the main ones are:

1. *Commodity item*—no differentiation at all; you cannot add value to the basic raw material, because all competitors are

selling the same thing, so you must put some added-value "envelope" around it with a different way of providing it. The airline flight is a differentiated product for the airline, but for the travel agent who sells the ticket to the customer it is a commodity to which the agent must add value; the customer can get it from any agency.

2. *Uniqueness*—a product with very few competitors or exact counterparts; in London you can take a tour of the neighborhood in which Jack the Ripper supposedly did his deeds.

3. *Features and functions*—an item distinguished by its usefulness or functional appeal, such as a software program, an upscale stereo system, a camera, or an electronic doghouse.

4. *Physical quality*—something so well made, or made of such precious material, that it has special appeal, such as Waterford crystal, upscale automobiles, or hand-tailored suits.

5. *Style and trend*—fashion items that must keep up with latest trends, such as clothing, music, style-oriented magazines, or hair designs.

6. *Speed or timeliness*—high-speed delivery of parcels, fast-breaking news reporting, or placing orders for soybean futures contracts.

7. *Personal attention*—psychiatric care, occupational therapy or rehabilitation, investment advice, or root-canal work.

8. *Lifestyle or self-identification*—items used by the customer to express to others his or her life values, social status, prestige, or membership in an admired clique; includes high-end luxury cars, designer-name clothing, exclusive club memberships, and a hair stylist who does movie stars.

9. *Risk management*—items that create trust, confidence, or freedom from fear, such as insurance, burglar alarms, security services, high-risk medical procedures, or vitamin supplements.

10. *Informational value*—information sold for its sheer utility value, such as newsletters, on-line data services, investment advice, or legal advice.

There may be items in your business that don't fall neatly into these categories, or there may be items that bridge across two or more of them. The important thing is not to classify them, but to reflect carefully on the essential appeal of the item to the customer. Exploiting this appeal must become part of the business logic, and it must find its way into the strategic model.

Your Economic Logic

Your economic logic answers the question, How will we get profit and growth? It translates the logic of customer access and the product logic into a profit mechanism. Bear in mind that maximizing profit may not always be the single business objective. In some cases, it might be advisable to trade off profit for market share or other intermediate business objectives. Consequently, the economic logic might need to shift from time to time. Some of the most obvious options for your economic logic are:

1. *Market growth*—as customers multiply or natural demand increases, there is more total demand available to capitalize on. A rising tide lifts all boats.

2. *Market-share expansion*—gaining market share at the expense of other players.

3. *Demand creation*—communicating the benefits to people so well that they become customers; in the computer industry the early software packages, however primitive at the time, made the computer a plausible asset to many people. Before the arrival of commercial software, it was just a technical curiosity.

4. *Acquisitions*—absorbing sales volume or market share by acquiring other firms already doing business in the sector you want to occupy.

5. *Vertical integration*—operating at more than one step along the value chain from raw material to finished product; a steel firm may acquire the mining operation that supplies it; a film production company might acquire a chain of movie theaters.

6. *Price dominance*—the right to charge a higher price than your competitors, due to some offsetting added-value advan-

tage; or the ability to charge lower prices than they can bear, due to a superior cost structure or economies of scale.

7. *Cost performance*—having a specially advantageous cost structure that improves your profit, generates capital needed for growth, or enables you to withstand price wars.

Again, it makes sense to consider more than one of these avenues for economic logic, and to look for compatible combinations. Together with your customer logic and your product logic, your economic logic drives many of your strategic choices.

Your Structural Logic

Your structural logic describes your organizing approach—the infrastructure for value creation you have chosen for your enterprise. It should implement and support the combination of customer logic, product logic, and economic logic that works for you. Author and consultant Robert Tomasko makes a special point of this in his book *Rethinking the Corporation: The Architecture of Change*. He emphasizes the need to "organize around cross-cutting processes, not fiefdoms."[1]

It is not uncommon for an organization's structural logic to contradict or even undermine the other elements of its business logic. Some of the choices for the focus of your structural logic are:

1. *Product focus*—using a key product as the defining element of the operation; Cray Computers produces a few mega-computers per year, each one unique and each one selling for millions of dollars.

2. *Technology focus*—assigning lots of people to research, development, and implementation of new methods that will directly affect the product or service provided; a culture in which high-tech professional people have the strongest voices, get the most resources, and get ahead faster than others.

3. *Production focus*—concentrating on managing the production process so skillfully that it creates a competitive advantage through product quality or cost advantages; Motorola's

famous "six-sigma" manufacturing process for semiconductors and electronic products has earned it a world reputation in certain markets.

4. *Selling focus*—concentrating all energies on helping the customer decide to buy; Nordstrom department stores all have a strong selling focus underlying the "customer service" image; all floor employees are constantly scored on the sales volume they generate.

5. *Distribution focus*—getting things where they need to be, when they need to be there; the quintessential examples are Federal Express, UPS, DHL, TNT, and other parcel delivery companies.

6. *Cost-control focus*—an unwavering commitment to being the lowest-cost producer, not merely pursuing defensive cost-consciousness; the Price Club chain of discount retail stores moves huge amounts of merchandise through its giant, austere, hangarlike outlets, with very few employees assigned to product support, selling, or after-sales service.

7. *Information focus*—organizing around the creation, manipulation, and movement of information; for example, a research organization, a news-gathering organization, or a computer database service.

8. *Response-time focus*—gearing the whole operation to doing things quickly and on demand; includes paramedics, rush delivery services, news wire services, and crisis consultants.

9. *Personal-contact focus*—the customer-facing employees adding value to the basic item by their skills, knowledge, and attitudes about service; typical of hotels, hospitals, and massage parlors.

10. *Account-retention focus*—keeping the business of the key customers rather than having to compete for them time and again; includes stockbrokers, personal physicians, consulting firms, and bookmakers.

Testing Your Business Logic: Does It Make Sense?

Think about the way various combinations of the four sublogics go together. Clearly, not all combinations make sense. Some work better than others. Let's look at a few examples. Using a "Chinese menu" approach, we can see how some one option from each of the four categories combines with the others.

For example, the Price Club discount store chain, has roughly the following business logic:

- Customer logic—wide customer range, coupled with wide product range.
- Product logic—commodity, that is, useful products people can buy from many suppliers.
- Economic logic—price dominance, combined with cost performance; their prices are significantly lower than those of most specialty marketers.
- Structural logic—selling focus; they immerse the customer in an overwhelming selection of goods with prices posted conspicuously, provide huge shopping carts, and move them through the checkout stands quickly and efficiently.

For Price Club, the business logic hangs together. They do not try to be more than one thing. They make no attempt to imitate upscale marketers like Nordstrom or to use personal selling to move products. A customer can buy a computer or a fax machine or a television set for a low price but must know how to make his or her own choice from the items presented.

Let's look at another example, Nordstrom department stores. We could describe the business logic as:

- Customer logic—target market, here the upscale person who likes to shop in a luxurious environment.
- Product logic—lifestyle and self-identification; many people who shop at Nordstrom's like to let their friends know it.
- Economic logic—market share growth; Nordstrom typically does very well in its carefully selected locations, and there is room for significant growth from its base of about fifty stores.
- Structural logic—selling focus combined with personal-attention focus; Nordstrom people sell hard in a low-key way, often maintaining contact with their "clients" and

contacting them with information about new products and news of special sales.

Notice how vastly different the two forms of business logic are between Price Club and Nordstrom. Price Club customers would not expect to have a pianist entertaining them while they shop, nor would they expect a sales employee to escort them all over the store while they select their purchases. On the other hand, Nordstrom customers would not expect to hear brassy selling messages broadcast over the PA system, nor would they expect to push shopping carts around over bare concrete floors, maneuvering in and out of aisles stocked with mass-market branded merchandise. These are two different logics, and both work.

What happens when the logic doesn't work? What about a situation in which the company is trying to operate with a self-contradictory business logic? One of the major New York brokerage houses asked for a review of its business logic, because it was steadily losing business with its target market, the upscale, active investor. When we reviewed the business logic dispassionately, we found it looked something like this:

- Customer logic—target market; the most attractive segment of the investor population.
- Product logic—commodity; although one investment vehicle might be much better than another, all brokers sell all of them, so the broker cannot differentiate on the basis of the vehicle itself.
- Economic logic—price dominance; the brokerage wanted to be the "high-priced spread," that is, to charge premium commissions and not compete on price with the discount brokers.
- Structural logic—selling focus combined with account-retention focus; the brokers spent almost all of their time "dialing and smiling," with their compensation heavily tilted toward generating commissions from new sales or from "churning" assets in existing portfolios.

The flaw in the business logic was the attempt to combine a commodity logic, a price dominance logic, and a selling logic, in the hope of capturing an upscale target market. Although the company gave lip service in its advertising to the supposed added value of its research and advisory services, our customer interviews revealed that few customers knew what was available, few took advantage of it, and few considered it an important difference. In fact, most of the firm's investors simply called their broker and placed orders. Occasionally the broker would contact a customer with a sales pitch for a particular investment vehicle.

The company had not structured its business logic in such a way as to offer a credible reason why the customer should pay a full commission on an investment purchase when discount brokers were providing equal value at lower commission rates. Our research also indicated that brokers significantly overestimated customer loyalty, and that the majority of customers perceived no special value dealing with one particular broker or with this particular company.

This review of the business logic led the executives to reexamine the whole concept of their business and to revisit the issue of customer value, looking for a valid way to establish a competitive advantage.

One of the benefits of this model of business logic is that it enables the leaders of the enterprise to test the basic success premise of the business and to begin rethinking it if it doesn't have the promise of succeeding in the environment.

Note

1. Robert M. Tomasko, *Rethinking the Corporation: The Architecture of Change* (New York: AMACOM, 1993), p. 111.

Chapter 11

Model Building 104: The Customer Value Package

Business is what, if you don't have, you go out of.

Old Jewish proverb

The Infrastructure for Creating Customer Value

Now it's time to take a close look at the "delivery system," that is, the infrastructure used by the enterprise to create customer value. Another name for it is the customer interface. It is the total collection of people, systems, processes, and experiences that the customer comes into contact with in getting his or her needs met.

Although organizations are vastly different in the ways they interact with their customers, there are some basic recurring themes in those interactions. By looking at many different types of businesses and many kinds of customer interactions, we can discern a basic, generic framework for describing the interface. This *customer value package* is a multidimensional architecture for managing the customer's experience with the enterprise, and with the value it creates. The customer value package must be right if we hope to build in the customer's mind an impression of quality and value for money.

The Seven Components of the Customer Value Package

We can think of the customer value package as having seven more or less generic dimensions or aspects, as depicted in Figure 11-1.

Each business will have its unique version of each of the components, but they all have certain common aspects. Let's see how these seven components go together to form the infrastructure for delivery of customer value.

1. *Environmental*—the physical setting in which the customer experiences the product. It could be a hospital room, a bank lobby, an airplane cabin, a barber chair, a department store, the sidewalk in front of an automatic teller machine, a fitness center, or any of a limitless number of possibilities. In the case of service at a distance, the environment may be the customer's own premises, possibly augmented by the tele-

Figure 11-1.   The seven dimensions of the customer value package.

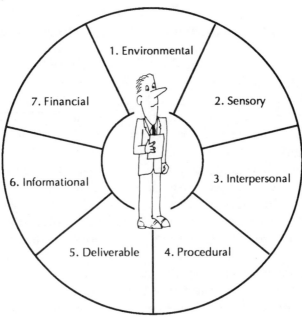

phone through which he or she makes contact with the business.

2. *Sensory*—the direct sensory experiences, if any, that the customer encounters. This component includes sights, sounds, flavors, physical sensations, pain or discomfort, emotional reactions, aesthetic features of an item of merchandise, and the psychological ambience of the customer environment.

3. *Interpersonal*—the interaction the customer has with employees or, in some cases, with other customers, as part of the total experience. This dimension includes friendliness, courtesy, helpfulness, physical appearance, and apparent competence at handling important tasks.

4. *Procedural*—the procedures you ask the customer to go through in doing business with you. They may include waiting, explaining his or her needs, filling out forms, providing information, going to various locations, and being subjected to physical manipulation or treatments.

5. *Deliverable*—anything the customer physically takes custody of during the service experience, even if only temporarily. It would certainly include an item of merchandise purchased, but it could also include the tray of food served on an airline or in a hospital. It might not always be a product in the conventional commercial sense, but the customer receives it nevertheless. Other examples are checkbooks, rented videotapes, menus, travel documents, and life jackets.

6. *Informational*—aspects of the customer experience that involve getting the information needed to function as a customer. This includes simple things like whether the signage in a facility enables the customer to figure out where to go, whether he or she can decipher the invoice or account statement, and whether the insurance policy is understandable. It can include critical factors like whether anyone has adequately explained the use of some item of equipment or whether the customers know what to expect of a critical medical procedure.

7. *Financial*—what the customer pays for the total experience. In most cases it's obvious: It's the price. In others, it may be less obvious. For example, an insurance company may pay the medical bills, but the customer is still aware of the price.

Analyzing Your Customer Value Package

Every enterprise should subject its customer value package to
continual and critical scrutiny, with the objective of constantly
improving it. Using the seven components just described, its
leaders can conduct a "value audit" of the customer interface
to see how well it performs. It is also important to get the direct
input of customers in this audit in order to discover defects or
opportunities not obvious to the leaders themselves. As a
practice exercise, prior to auditing your own customer value
package, consider the case of an automobile dealership. What
features of each value-delivery component deserve attention?

1. *Environmental.* The display lot, the showroom, the sales
floor, the reception area—what do they convey? Is the place
clean, attractive, professional-looking, inviting? Does it make
the prospective customer feel welcome and comfortable?

2. *Sensory.* Does the place "feel" like a decent place to do
business? Does the prospective customer have positive sensory
experiences? What does it feel like to sit inside the car? How
does it feel to drive it? Is it appealing to the eye?

3. *Interpersonal.* Are the people friendly, courteous, and
considerate? Do they attack the person who just wants to
browse, or do they respect his or her dignity? During a sales
conversation, do they build the customer's trust and confidence, or do they make him or her feel uncomfortable with
pressure tactics?

4. *Procedural.* Are employees easy to do business with?
Are they flexible, or do they insist the customer follow their
procedures? Do they minimize the paperwork?

5. *Deliverable.* The car itself: Is it what the customer actually ordered? Does everything work? Is everything clean? Are
the documents all in order?

6. *Informational.* Does the customer fully understand the
terms of the purchase? The warranty? The procedures for
correcting defects? The maintenance schedule? Does someone
take the customer for a ride in the car, and make sure he or
she understands all the controls?

7. *Financial.* Does the customer feel the price is fair? Does he or she fully understand the financial arrangements, including extra charges, insurance, and financing charges? Does the customer feel he or she received real value for the money paid?

How about other customer value packages? Here are some other examples to consider in training yourself to analyze things from the perspective of the customer's experience:

- Getting a loan from a bank
- Spending a day at Disneyland
- Sending a package by overnight delivery
- Spending a weekend at a hotel
- Attending classes at a university
- Shopping in a bookstore
- Having surgery in a hospital
- Renting a tuxedo for a wedding
- Taking a vacation on a cruise boat
- Applying for a permit at a city department

Once you feel fairly familiar with the thinking process behind the customer value model, think about your own busi-

Figure 11-2. The customer value matrix.

Customer Value Factors

	CVF-1	CVF-2	CVF-3	CVF-4	CVF-5	CVF-6
Environmental						
Sensory						
Interpersonal						
Deliverance						
Procedural						
Informational						
Financial						

ness. What does your interface look like, feel like, and act like to your customers? Can you say with confidence that the design of your value package fully reflects the customer value model that's the basis for your business? Or did it just grow and evolve, reflecting the convenience of the organization more than the convenience of the customer?

Figure 11-2, the customer value matrix, shows how to nnect the customer value model (CVM) to the customer value package (CVP). By cross-charting each of the factors of the CVM against each of the seven dimensions of the CVP, you can zero in on the areas that offer opportunities for improvement and for creating competitive advantage.

The next step coming up in our discussion of the strategy development process is the strategic gap analysis, in which you compare your present customer value package with the ideal one you feel is necessary for success. Then you can go to work on redesigning or improving it to close the performance gap.

Chapter 12

Strategic Gap Analysis: What's the "Delta"?

Chance favors the prepared mind.

Louis Pasteur

The "Delta": The Disparity Between What is and What Ought to Be

Reviewing the basic strategy formulation process presented in Figure 4-2, we can see that the next step after building the strategic success model is the strategic gap analysis. Assuming that we have crafted a valid vision statement, mission statement, and core values or philosophy in response to the environmental scan, organizational scan, and opportunity scan; that we have linked up with the customer value model; that we have developed the business logic and strategy; and finally that we have now defined or redefined the customer value package that constitutes our competitive offering, it is time to ask, "So what?"

We have to figure out whether the enterprise as it works now actually delivers value as it will need to. And if not, we have to figure out how to bring it into line with the ideal strategic success model we have developed.

The Greek letter delta, represented in its capital form by a simple triangle sitting on its base, is a symbol engineers and mathematicians like to use as a shorthand reference for talking about the difference between two variables. Deep inside the workings of the computer on board the astronauts' spaceship there is a delta—a signal that measures the difference between where the ship is supposed to be going and where it actually is going. The computer's job is to redirect the rockets so that the delta goes toward zero.

Think about it carefully and you'll realize that a spaceship spends more time off course than on course. It is only perfectly on course for short periods, and the computer must constantly measure the delta and correct its course back toward the intended one. If the ship doesn't have a course to follow, or if it doesn't know whether it's on the correct course, there is little chance it will arrive at the destination.

The leaders of any enterprise need to know about their own delta. In strategy thinking, the delta is the difference between what is and what ought to be. It should be the driving consciousness behind the choice of various strategic maneuvers, competitive actions, investments, new developments, organizational changes, and many other actions aimed at reorienting the enterprise toward its destination.

In quite a few organizations, the planning processes wander off course somewhere and don't ever get to the gap-analysis stage. They may start with flowery, grandiose strategy statements and then plunge into specific action plans that have no apparent relationship to the supposed strategic success model. Acquisitions, investments, new-product developments, and the like often become elements of the operational plan without ever being tested to see whether they are the best options for fulfilling the concept of the northbound train. If you don't take your strategy thinking seriously, you end up with a bunch of nice words and a random collection of disconnected actions and projects that somebody thinks would be nice to do. The strategic concept must show up in the action planning, or else why go through all of that effort?

"Foreign" Strategy and "Domestic" Strategy

There is no standard recipe for thinking through the gap analysis, because each enterprise has its own unique strategic success model and current business situation, and consequently its own unique gaps. But as a minimum, its leaders need to consider gaps in both "foreign" and "domestic" dimensions, that is, what has to be done in coping with the outside environment and what has to be done to develop the internal environment, culture, and people.

In some cases, the demands of the external environment may be so pressing that everyone has to give a great deal of attention to them. In other cases, both environments require close attention. But in still others, the internal environment may present the greater demands and opportunities. In no case should the domestic issues be treated as secondary, or as footnotes to the "real" business issues. They are just as real and just as entitled to attention as the more conventionally understood external issues. Both internal and external gaps can constrain the ability of the enterprise to create its intended value.

It is often helpful to divide the thinking process of gap analysis into two steps. The first step is figuring out what the gaps are and coming to an agreement on the few critical ones that need primary attention. The second step is identifying the kinds of action options to be considered for closing the gaps. This is the connecting point with the next stage of the strategy formulation model, which is action planning.

What, actually, is a gap? What does one look like? What does the delta mean in practical terms? The answer is: A strategic gap is a shortfall between the value-creation capability required for success in a certain area and the organization's current capability in that area. For example, if the strategic concept includes having customer access in a certain country and you don't currently have it, that's a gap. There may be various ways of achieving it, but until you recognize it as a gap and get to work on it, nothing will happen.

Another gap might be a significant hole in your product range, compared to what you believe is needed to play in a certain market. To close the gap, you might not necessarily have to develop those products with your own assets; it might be possible to acquire the rights to market someone else's products if they exist. Another gap might be market recognition; you need to have more customers aware of what you can do for them.

Internal gaps also deserve attention. Suppose your strategic success model calls for having a superior cost structure that allows you to outprice most of your competitors. If your current cost structure is nothing special, you have an internal gap. You'll have to figure out how to change that cost structure significantly, maybe even redesigning much of the process behind it.

There may be an internal gap caused by a deficit in the skills of your people. If certain skills are required to make your strategic success model work and the people don't have those skills, then that area calls for action. A more challenging gap might arise from the strategic need to present a unified, "seamless" interface to customers who do business with you across the country or across national borders. If the organization works like a batch of regional tribes and does not currently enable the customer to do business conveniently, that's an internal gap.

Some of the gaps you identify may be fairly simple and may invite straightforward action. Others may be much harder to close. In particular, gaps that arise from deeply rooted aspects of your organizational culture may present tougher challenges than you anticipate. In any case, it is important to take an organized approach to gap analysis, and to make sure you are working on the gaps that have the greatest effect on the ability of the enterprise to implement its strategic success model.

Closing the Gap With Strategic Initiatives

Think of a strategic action initiative, whether directed externally or internally, as an effort mounted to close one or more strategic gaps. This might be a somewhat different use of terminology than you will find in other approaches to strategy thinking. Most people tend to think of the term *strategic* as applying only to the external environment. However, in this discussion it applies to actions that have a *payoff* in the external environment, regardless of whether the focus of those actions is external or internal.

Externally directed strategic initiatives might include forming alliances or coventures with other compatible enterprises, launching a large-scale advertising or promotion campaign, withdrawing from certain areas of the competitive field, opening up physical offices to establish psychological presence in a business environment, introducing a "continuity" product that gives you long-term access to certain customers, and acquiring a firm that operates in a sector you need to gain access to.

Internally directed strategic initiatives might include shifting certain costly activities to an outsourcing basis, restructuring geographic territories to improve coordination and customer access, reengineering your organizational systems to simplify them, changing your product development process to radically shorten time-to-market, and rearranging certain customer-contact processes to make them more customer-friendly.

The range of creative strategic initiatives is virtually limitless. Scan through any business magazine and notice the kinds of changes firms are making in their attempts to improve their success possibilities. Pick any one news account and try to visualize the discussion that must have taken place among the leaders of the company that led to the selection of this particular action. How would you describe the gap they seem to be trying to close? Are there other initiatives they might take similar to this one or supportive of this one? How valid do you think their chosen initiative is with regard to the apparent gap?

In the next chapter we will deal with the action planning process that enables you to choose the few critical gap-closing initiatives that will make the most sense for your enterprise.

Chapter 13

Action Planning

Take care of the means,
and the end will take care of itself.

Mohandas K. Gandhi

The more effective the *thinking* process is at the strategic level, the less elaborate the *planning* process needs to be at the tactical, operational levels. Too many organizations waste the valuable time and energy of their tactical leaders by forcing them to go through meaningless rituals under the guise of planning. As mentioned in Chapter 4, much of what people in bureaucratic organizations think of as planning is little more than extrapolated budgeting. And much of that is unnecessary.

The action planning step in the strategy formulation process presents an opportunity to focus energies carefully and thoughtfully. It is a chance to decide what few things we are going to do, and do outstandingly well. If we call the shots with style and grace at this point, we can be much more confident than otherwise that the strategic success model can become reality.

The action planning step, if well carried out, has three useful outcomes:

1. A set of meaningful *business targets* for the upcoming performance period
2. A few well-chosen *key result areas* that can channel

actions and energies toward closing the strategic gap and meeting the business targets

3. A very few well-chosen *adaptive goals* under the key result areas, which serve as aiming points for evaluating how well we've focused our energies on results

If these three outcomes provide an effective framework for moving forward, then almost any reasonable tactical planning process will probably work. If they do not, then the most elaborate planning process will be a mere exercise in bureaucracy.

So action planning is all about translation. It's about translating the message from the visionary strategy language into the more concrete language of outcomes and responsibilities. It's about interpreting the promise of the strategic success model into everyday life. It's about "reducing great ideas to crude deeds."

Setting Business Targets That Actualize the Strategic Model

Refer to the basic strategic hierarchy shown in Figure 4-1, and remind yourself that the business targets, key result areas (KRAs), and adaptive goals are unique to your enterprise. Most likely they are unique to a particular planning period or strategic phase in the life of the enterprise. The key to using them effectively is traceability back up the strategic hierarchy; that is, they should clearly actualize the strategic success model.

There isn't much confusion about most of the typical kinds of business targets used in most types of commercial organizations. For a government or nonprofit enterprise they may, of course, be quite specialized to its mission and environment. But for the most part, they usually include targets such as gross revenue, gross margin, gain in revenue or margin above the prior period, market share or share improvement, return on invested assets, earnings per share, and various operational measures like occupancy rate for hotels or hospitals, productivity in terms of revenue per full-time employee, or salary multipliers for consulting or accounting firms. Other kinds of businesses might measure new customers signed up, new service contracts captured, or booked backlog of business as of year's end.

It is usually better to have a few very compelling business targets rather than a long list of measures. It's easier to get people to remember and focus on the few than on the many. And if well selected, a few critical business targets can drive the operation in the right direction, accounting for most of the rest of the measures anyway.

Defining Key Result Areas

The concept of the key result area, or KRA, is one of the valuable holdovers from the old days in which management by objectives, or MBO, was the theology of business. MBO was widely misunderstood and misapplied, unfortunately, but some of its key precepts were timeless. One of them is the idea of simply identifying a few broad areas for concentrating attention over the upcoming performance period, and using these categories, or key result areas, as a means to keep all efforts connected and focused.

A key result area, in simplest terms, is a dimension for change management, either externally or internally directed, that needs action in order to close the strategic gap between the current state of the enterprise and the ideal state defined by the strategic success model, that is, the hierarchy. A few high-impact key result areas are better than many. Three is a practical number; any more than five tends to indicate a weak sense of focus or an attempt to do too many things.

As with business targets, key result areas must be unique to your own enterprise and focused on what you want to accomplish during the upcoming performance period. Note that, by this definition, a KRA is *not* a standard category of operating results, such as revenue, profit, or unit volume. Those are the business targets. A KRA, by contrast, governs an area of focus for *change management*. It is not business as usual; it is an imperative for changing something about the business.

As mentioned in a previous example, if your organization's cost structure is out of whack with the pricing pattern dictated by your business logic, then you might identify changing the cost structure as a key result area. The strategic initiatives, or action areas under that KRA, should all focus on that purpose. With this particular example, note that setting a KRA for changing the cost structure is not necessarily the same as setting one for cost reduction. Cost reduction can result in eliminating or deferring expenditures that might still have to be made eventually, whereas changing the cost structure might mean a more fundamental change in the organization. The choice of words can make a big difference.

A well-stated key result area is:

• *Focused.* It deals with a single selected dimension of change and change management; it does not try to rope too many problems into one statement. Examples: "Launch new catalog marketing operation," "acquire new third-party products," or "retain critical talent."

• *High impact.* It's the right place to go to work; it highlights a really important action area that can have a significant payoff. Examples: "overseas partnerships," "new customer-access channels," or "key-customer retention."

• *Well named.* "Employee motivation," "employee involvement," and "employee participation" can mean three different things; you have to think carefully about the message conveyed by the label you affix to the KRA.

The place to start thinking about which KRAs you want to set is back with the strategic gap analysis. Each of the gaps you have identified begins to suggest some actions, or at least lines of effort, which might be appropriate for closing them. By thinking of the overall delta, that is, the difference between the present state of the enterprise and the ideal state defined by the strategic success model, you can begin to discern the patterns that seem to connect the various gaps together.

For example, if the news from the competitive arena tells you that your organization is losing business because your various field operations don't cooperate or respond quickly enough to customer demands, then some sort of teamwork premise seems to be called for. If the evidence is also clear that field offices can't respond because of insufficient support or timeliness or response on the part of the home office, teamwork seems to be shaping up as a possible KRA. Other findings, when considered in this context, may confirm that view. If so, setting a KRA around teamwork would probably be a good way to organize a number of initiatives into a pattern everybody can understand and relate to.

A KRA, once it goes up "on the wall," should have a certain obviousness about it. It should have a categorical name and a focus that convey the sense of a serious attack on problems, opportunities, deficiencies, or gaps that are important.

Just as important, a KRA should not be selected for socially acceptable reasons, for example, because it seems like we "should" have one on employee development, or customer focus, or teamwork, or whatever is trendy. There should only be a few key result areas, or else they are not really key. Each one is too precious to be wasted on a vague category with a nice name. Each one has to count, and it has to pull energy and resources in a very important and valuable direction.

In an executive strategy retreat meeting, the assembly of the key result areas is a very important test point for evaluating the success of the strategy formulation process so far. If the KRAs have an obvious sense of rightness about them, if they clearly relate to achieving the northbound train concept the leaders have developed, and if there is strong consensus around going forward with them, then there is a fairly good chance the team has put together a success model and a way to implement it that hold promise for at least the near future of the enterprise.

Setting the Few Critical Adaptive Goals

And finally, the action planning step results in a few carefully chosen goals as aiming points under the key result areas. This, too, is an adaptation of the MBO thinking process. Once you have identified a particular key result area, the trick is to create one or two well-formed goal statements that represent significant accomplishments in that area. Again, a few simple goals, perhaps one in each area, are better than many. If you have five key result areas and five goals under each KRA, you have twenty-five goals to aim for; this is probably not a plausible plan. Far better would be to have only one really key goal under each KRA. People can keep them in mind more easily, you can manage progress toward them more effectively, and you are far more likely to achieve them.

A well-formed goal statement is:

• *Verifiable.* You know it when you've reached it; there should be some agreed-on criteria, whether objective and numerical or subjective and qualitative, for assessing progress toward it and concluding that it has been achieved. Example: "We will have signed coventure agreements with business partners in each of our target foreign markets by year's end."

• *Achievable.* It is realistically doable under reasonable circumstances. Setting impossible goals only demoralizes people, but setting worthwhile goals that are achievable contributes toward an achieving mind-set. Example: "We will have the new software up and operating in all customer-contact departments by midyear, and in the rest of the departments by year's end."

• *Valuable.* It is a worthwhile thing to aim for; achieving it brings important benefits that everyone can recognize and appreciate. Example: "All employees will be familiar with the vision, mission, core values, and basic business direction of the firm by the end of July."

• *Ownable.* The people who have to commit to its attainment must be able to see it as belonging to them in some way. Perhaps everybody has to do certain things for the overall goal to be reached; perhaps certain people have to take the lead—in any case, it has to belong to somebody. Example: "In all divisions, 100 percent of the employees will complete the customer-focus training program within twelve months after it commences."

• *Actionable.* The goal must translate clearly into some indicated action or group of actions. It is not enough for it to float before the eyes of interested bystanders; they must be able to figure out what they have to do to make it come true.

Example: "We will have the customer-perception survey system set up and delivering regular reports by X date."

Remember here, again, that the adaptive goals are *not* the standard operating measures or business results. They are the goals set for the change-management process. Tracing once again the process of Figure 4-1, we see the logical flow from the strategic success model with its vision, mission, values, customer value model, and customer value package, through the business logic and strategy and the setting of the business results. The strategic initiatives coming out of the gap analysis lead us to defining the key result areas, and each KRA calls for a few critical adaptive goals that help close the gap between the ideal strategic success model and the current state of the enterprise.

Once you've done all of that, you're still not finished. The most important part is still to come: strategy deployment, as explained in the next chapter.

Chapter 14

Strategy Deployment

A leader is best when people barely know that he
exists.
Not so good when people obey and acclaim him,
Worst when they despise him.
Fail to honor people,
They fail to honor you.
But of a good leader, who talks little,
When his work is done, his aim fulfilled,
They will all say "We did this ourselves."

Witter Bynner, *The Way of Life According to Lao-tzu*

Don't Keep It a Secret

If we were to stand at the entrance of the building housing the
operations of any randomly selected large company and inter-
view the employees arriving for their day's work, what percentage of them do you think could explain accurately what
the organization does, what it stands for, and what factors are
critical to its—and their—success? How many could at least
paraphrase the written vision, mission, and declared values of
the enterprise? How many would have a working knowledge
of the customer value model and the key business priorities?
How many would care?

What if we interviewed the employees of your enterprise?
How many of them would understand the big picture?

These questions reveal an underlying value judgment: that employees *should* know the big picture and their place in it. Clearly, many executives don't believe in that, judging by the number of organizations in which the "average working stiff" knows very little except his or her own job tasks. It's quite remarkable how many employees of large organizations haven't a clue what happens to their work after it leaves their hands. If they don't know what the people in the next building do, it isn't likely they know very much about the overall enterprise.

Many executives consciously or unconsciously hold to the view that the employees are there to do what they're told and it's the job of their managers to tell them. The underlying assumptions of Western management have always reinforced the image of the employee as a doer, not a thinker. Deploying the strategy throughout the organization implies that its leaders believe people can create greater value if they know more, and that they indeed do want to know more. As a leader of your particular enterprise, you have to ask yourself how you feel and what you believe regarding human intelligence.

Executive Evangelism: Creating Ownership for the Direction

The late Sam Walton, founder of the enormously successful Wal-Mart chain of variety stores, could often be seen wandering into his stores to have a chat with the employees. He'd stroll through the aisles, discuss the products and services with the customers, and talk at length with the store and department managers about the Wal-Mart way of doing things. Often he would grab the microphone at the service desk and give all the store employees a Sam Walton pep talk in his own homespun style. Most of them felt a special lift, a kind of affirmation of the value of what they were doing, when the "old man" showed up.

It wasn't a very complicated message; it wasn't rocket science, or market share statistics, or rules and regulations. It was always just about the same simple message: We're all here to create value for our customers; you can be proud of what you do and what you contribute; and if there is anything your managers or I ought to be doing to help you do your job better, we want you to tell us about it.

Sam Walton was an executive evangelist. He was, to adapt the term used in Chapter 2, a "human logo." His mere presence had become, for Wal-Mart people, a symbolic message that triggered a constellation of ideas and feelings in them. They associated the logo with the superordinate message of value creation.

Although he was a multibillionaire, he preferred to drive around in an old pickup truck, and he often worked out of a very modest office in a little strip mall. He didn't convey the impression of a distant, wealthy, high-powered capitalist; to Wal-Mart employees he was just Sam. And his message was simple and unarguable: We're all here to create value.

Executive evangelism has always been in short supply. We could use lots more of it in the business world. I'm sure we would see much less cynicism on the part of working people, much less apathy, much less dishonesty, and much more enthusiasm and commitment to creating value if they felt their executives really knew who they were, understood their struggles, and showed that they believed in them. The sense of disconnectedness and alienation many people feel in their careers is part of the legacy of Western management: the view of people as things rather than as humans with needs.

Curiously, executives who tend to view their customers as things, as replaceable commodities coming along in a queue, and as statistical units of business, tend to be the same ones who view the workers as "capital." Both ideas come from the same impersonal value system. Conversely, executives who have a compelling interest in and focus on seeing customers as individual human beings with needs, and who keep the focus on creating customer value, tend to be the same ones who create a leadership climate that values all of the people in the organization as individuals.

Feargal Quinn, founder and chief executive of the SuperQuinn chain of food markets in Dublin, exemplifies this positive customer focus in everything he does. On a typical day, you can find him behind the checkout counter in one of the stores, helping the clerks bag groceries during the rush period, walking the aisles helping customers find the items they want, explaining how the shops make their own sausage, or helping the stock clerks keep the shelves full.

In his book *Crowning the Customer*, Quinn says:

> Apart from the time I devote to customer panels, I spend about half my time every week on the floor of our shops, meeting customers. Many chief executives would consider this a waste of their time, but I don't. I never come away from the shop floor without having learned something new.
>
> One of my favourite chores is helping to pack the customers' bags at the checkouts.
>
> Menial? Not at all!
>
> It is an excellent place to meet customers, and the fact that I have something to do as I talk to them means that conversations are more relaxed and natural.
>
> Some top executives subscribe to what I call the "Royal Tour Syndrome." But that's not the way to meet customers.
>
> Customers are not troops to be reviewed; they are people to be served. The best way to meet customers is to roll up your sleeves and do the job.[1]

Quinn has his own philosophy about what executives should be doing:

> I always feel sorry for any company in which a finance man takes over the top position. I know the company is going to go downhill. People who don't understand customer value are no good at running businesses. They think the business is just a big machine that runs on money. They don't understand that a business is a way real people create value for other real people. If you understand that, you can make almost any business succeed.[2]

Even though executive evangelism is in short supply, it is still alive and well in a number of enterprise leaders. Bill Marriott, chairman of the multibillion-dollar Marriott Corporation, spends up to 25 percent of his time traveling around North America, Europe, and other regions to visit the people in the company's hotel and food service facilities. I've seen him walk into a hotel and show people that he has all the time in the world to talk to them and listen to their views about what they're doing. He will walk into virtually every department in a hotel, shaking hands with cooks, maids, desk clerks, bell service people, maintenance workers, and floor cleaners. The effect is absolutely electric. "Here I am," thinks a housekeeper, "an ordinary working person, shaking hands with the chairman of the board of the Marriott Corporation." It may seem cornball to many executives and administratively minded people, but to the person shaking hands with Marriott it's a high-powered experience.

At every opportunity, Marriott says to his managers, "Take care of the employees and they'll take care of the customers." He acknowledges that one critical dimension of his role is to serve as a symbol for the customer value message. When he shows up, his presence itself is the message. Whatever he says only adds detail to the basic message, which is "We're all here to create value." As Sam Walton was, Bill Marriott is a living logo.

Not all executives are comfortable with the evangelistic role, but nearly all can offer some semblance of it just by being who they are. They don't need acting lessons or video coaching, or practice in exhorting the troops. They simply need to understand and acknowledge the tremendous effect that a message can have when it is brought to people by a person with high authority. It takes on a special meaning and weight not possible when it simply comes out on a memo or poster. Executive evangelists understand that a handshake from the boss is a powerful message, regardless of the words that go with it.

Less Is More: The Power of a Simple Message

Compare these two statements of common cause by two very different business organizations, both of which you may recall from Chapters 7 and 9:

Hershey Foods Corporation

Hershey Foods Corporation's Mission is to become a major diversified food company and a leading company in every aspect of our business as:

• The number one confectionery company in North America, moving toward worldwide confectionery market share leadership.
• A respected and valued supplier of high quality, branded, consumer food products in North America and selected international markets.

Microsoft Corporation

Our vision is a computer on every desk and in every home, running Microsoft software.

There is a lot to get across in crafting a message that expresses the common cause for a major enterprise, but there is also tremendous value in simplicity. This is one of the challenges in putting together the overall message for the people of the enterprise, and in deploying it throughout the organization.

The message can be so simple and inane that it becomes a platitude. In that case, it isn't likely to gain much acceptance or have much influence. On the other hand, if the message is complex and verbose, however informative, it will be very difficult to communicate and difficult to bring to life. So the leaders of the enterprise have to choose a point somewhere along the spectrum from ultrasimple to complex. This is a decision about what can work best in the culture they're trying to influence.

The Australian Gas Light Company, renamed the Natural Gas Company a few years ago, faced a similar challenge in deploying their customer-focused strategy for the business. CEO Len Bleasel, a well-respected leader who had come up through the ranks from his starting job as a plumber, realized the message had to be simple. But it also had to be focused. He says:

> I was sure we wouldn't get far with a bunch of customer-is-king platitudes. Australians don't go for that kind of stuff. But we did have a simple strategic objective. We were going after market share in the energy business. Our future, and the future of everyone in the company, depended on having more customers decide to hook up to natural gas. So that was our northbound train; that was the concept we wanted to deploy throughout the organization.

Bleasel gave the mission to Grant King, at that time general manager of the company's Sydney operations, and a small task force of thinkers. They were asked to work out a way to dramatize the message to the company's 2,500 people. They boiled it down to a very simple message: "Everything we do must help people choose natural gas." And the first three words, "Everything we do," became the tagline for the initiative.

Every employee went through a two-day workshop experience called the "Everything We Do" program. During the workshop, each person received a small booklet that explained what "everything we do" meant, in broad terms and to him or her as an individual. It explained the basics of the gas business, what the strategy was, and what the strategic goal called for in terms of the number of new customers they needed to win. This particular choice for their way of deploying the strategy worked extremely well, and still plays a key part in the company's thinking at all levels.

One of the foremost examples in the world of a company that has deployed its basic northbound train message throughout its organization is Disney, and in particular the Disneyland parks. The Disneyland business concept starts with a show business premise, in the form of an ongoing show in which the audience mixes with the performers. The basic value premise of the Disneyland experience is fun and fantasy delivered in a theatrical environment. That may sound simple, but when you explore the way Disney leaders have worked it into all the nooks and crannies of the organization, you can't help but be impressed.

Disney employees get the message constantly: You are not simply working at a "theme park," you are participating in a show. All of the operational vocabulary reinforces the show business spirit. There are no employees, only *cast members*. After all, every show has a cast. There is no personnel department; there is a casting department. They do not "hire people for jobs"; they cast them for roles. The cast members do not wear "uniforms"; they wear costumes. They are never to refer to the paying guests as a "crowd," but rather as an "audience." When someone is taking a break, he or she is "offstage" and is not to be seen by the audience. When the break is over, the cast member goes back "onstage." The language of show business is everywhere.

If you've ever visited one of the Disney parks, you have probably noticed how complete and all-encompassing the show business format is. Nothing is permitted to contradict it. From the overall design of the park down to the smallest detail, everything is crafted to convey the same message: You can go back to your childhood and enjoy a carefree day living as you always wanted to live. All cast members are expected to contribute to this seamless experience of fantasy and enjoyment. There is no room for a bored, burned-out, customer-hostile worker.

Even the overnight cleanup workers have a noble mission: When the park opens again the next morning, everything should look just as it did on the first opening day. Everything should be magically transformed to its original brand-new condition. They know what it takes to achieve that, and they know that nothing less will be acceptable.

The effect is in the details. For example, you will never see two Disney employees on a break, leaning against a wall and smoking. You will never see them strolling in the entrance gate in jeans, with their costumes over their shoulders. They prepare for their performance in an underground world that the guest never sees and probably never imagines. When a cast member goes "onstage," he or she usually just appears from behind a tree, steps out unobtrusively from an unnoticed door, or otherwise blends into the flow of humanity. In short, they are never out of character within view of the audience.

Isn't that how any good theatrical performance should work? The essence of theater is focus and deception. The cast must focus the attention of the audience on the performance itself, all the while concealing the backstage apparatus that creates it. Although Disney's cast members are expected to use originality and creativity in handling guest problems, nevertheless certain parts of their roles are very strictly defined. In terms of Peters and Waterman's "simultaneous loose and tight properties," they play their roles according to the script. There is room for interpretation, but no room for messing around with the script.

The essential business concept tolerates no contradictions, no distractions, and no compromises. Although very few businesses should imitate the actual operation of the Disney parks, most can learn a great deal about focus and concentration from them.

Clearly, there is no one message or format that everyone should feel obligated to use. Every enterprise is unique, and so are the kinds of messages that can animate its culture. All through the strategy formulation process, however, the leaders need to keep in mind that they will eventually need to dramatize and communicate the northbound train concept they are crafting. That realization can have a big impact on the way they choose to organize it and articulate it.

Helping the Organization Learn

Deploying the strategy means more than helping people know what the common cause is, and what train they're being asked to ride. It also means helping them get a clear idea of their own contributions to the success of the enterprise. This involves helping them interpret the grand vision into a focus for action at their levels.

One very effective way to do this is by helping department managers develop their own northbound train concepts, based on their understanding of the contribution their units should be making to the overall enterprise. By helping each unit

manager, and especially each middle manager, think of his or
her unit as an enterprise within the overall enterprise, you can
make the overall concept come alive in everyday work.

Just as the overall organization has a vision, mission, and
core values, just as it operates with a valid customer value
model and a clearly defined customer value package, and just
as it has a business logic that drives its priorities, so too should
the internal business unit have the same things.

This is the approach being taken by more and more organizations as the need for greater customer focus and clarity of
business direction becomes ever more imperative. For example,
the Queen's Medical Center, a 144-year-old hospital in Honolulu, used the Customer Value Business Planning process at all
department levels. It began with the Materiel Services Department, under the leadership of Bill Kennett, who wanted all 500
of his employees to have a common cause: service to their
internal customers.

In Kennett's department, we guided the leaders of such
units as housekeeping, food services, purchasing and stores,
surgical supply, patient transportation, printing, and laundry
through a series of workshops on customer value business
planning, and they came out with their own strategy models.
Each unit conducted focus group research with their various
internal customers, that is, the employees in other groups that
depended on them for services. Using this research to fashion
their own local customer value models, they then developed
vision, mission, and value statements and began to develop
customer feedback systems to help them find ways to create
more value for the organization.

In Australia's Department of Administrative Services, we
have helped leaders of all business units to use customer value
business-planning methods to transform a government agency
into a new breed of enterprise: a customer-focused provider of
services to public sector organizations, operating on commercial principles. According to Executive General Manager Ross
Divitt:

> We understood early on that the transformation we
> were trying to make would have to go deep into the
> organization, and that it would have to touch every-

body in some way. Once we developed the basic strategic model, we immediately began taking it to all levels and helping managers interpret it in their own operations.

Another of the most impressive examples I've seen of executive leadership committed to helping the organization learn is in the Brazilian health insurance company Amil. Chief executive Edson de Godoy Bueno and his partners, who built the company from nothing to one of the largest in its industry in just seven years, have committed themselves to educating their employees as part of their growth strategy. According to Edson, as he prefers to be called:

> We believe absolutely in the value of learning and education. I spend a great deal of my time talking to the employees at all levels, and to their managers, about our mission as a Brazilian company, and about what they can do to make their own futures positive and fulfilling.
> Here in Brazil, we have many people who need to learn basic skills so they can get ahead. It is our responsibility as corporate leaders, I believe, to help educate them. We have created many programs here in the company, and I am absolutely sure this is one of the critical factors in the success of Amil.

Amil's growth rate is virtually unprecedented among Brazilian firms, and the company has shown outstanding financial results in the toughest of times. Not only does the company make extensive use of employee training, but it expects its leaders at all levels to be current on the latest management thinking from all over the world. They have created their own internal M.B.A. program, with a curriculum focused on the needs and problems of Amil in particular and Brazil in general. The professors in the program are all Amil executives.

Amil brings leading foreign speakers on various aspects of management to Brazil to present their ideas to its managers and employees. Then they thoroughly dissect and analyze each message and make specific action plans for implementing as many of the ideas as possible. Edson must practice what he preaches: The position title on his business card is "Chairman and Training Manager."

In Chapter 6, on the organizational scan, we explored the question of whether the enterprise can operate as a learning organization, whether it can sense and adapt to challenges in its environment by changing itself. Learning, in this sense, calls for all the people in the organization, at all levels, to be willing and able to review their worlds, both exterior and interior, and to question everything they do in terms of its contribution to value. This continual questioning, rethinking, and reinventing process keeps the organization from getting arthritic and fossilized and enables it to get ahead of changes in its environment rather than be victimized by them. Strategy deployment is the essential driving force in that learning process.

Success Is Never Final, and Neither Is the Strategy

I've often quoted J. W. "Bill" Marriott as saying, "Success is never final." It's one of the most useful reminders I can think of that tells the leaders of any enterprise they have to keep reinventing it over time. Failing to do that is what has trapped many large corporations these days in some very unpleasant circumstances.

In many ways, the Western habit of planning on an annualized basis contributes to annualized and ritualized thinking. Annual strategic plans, annual operating budgets, annual performance reviews, and annual reports tend to cause executives to think of strategy formulation as something you do according to a schedule rather than something you do continuously. Because of the pressure of near-field events, many executives don't have time to prepare properly for the annual strategy retreat. If that happens, the creative possibilities are already reduced to a fraction of what they could be.

If executives think strategically all the time, working with both near-field and far-field issues, they will be gathering useful information, cooking up provocative ideas, identifying interesting opportunities, and provoking ongoing discussion and debate about everything. The annual strategy gathering is the chance to make something useful out of everything they've discovered, learned, and thought about through the year.

Strategic thinking, after all, is a process of educated guesswork. It is neither all science nor all art; maybe it's a scientific art, or maybe it's an artistic science. There is no divinely inspired truth to be discovered in charting the destiny of any enterprise. There is only the most enlightened concept for success that is possible given the information, energy, and talent applied to the issues. It requires a certain degree of humility, a willingness to question one's own certainty, and at the same time the willingness to commit fully to a common cause and get on with it.

But above all, there *must be* a northbound train, however difficult the process of defining it. The people who give their energies, their ideas, their personal commitment, and, in many cases, their careers to the enterprise deserve no less.

Notes

1. Feargal Quinn, *Crowning the Customer: How to Become Customer-Driven* (Dublin: The O'Brien Press, 1990). This book can be ordered from The O'Brien Press, 20 Victoria Road, Dublin 6 Ireland.
2. Ibid.

Index